I AM

Gandhi

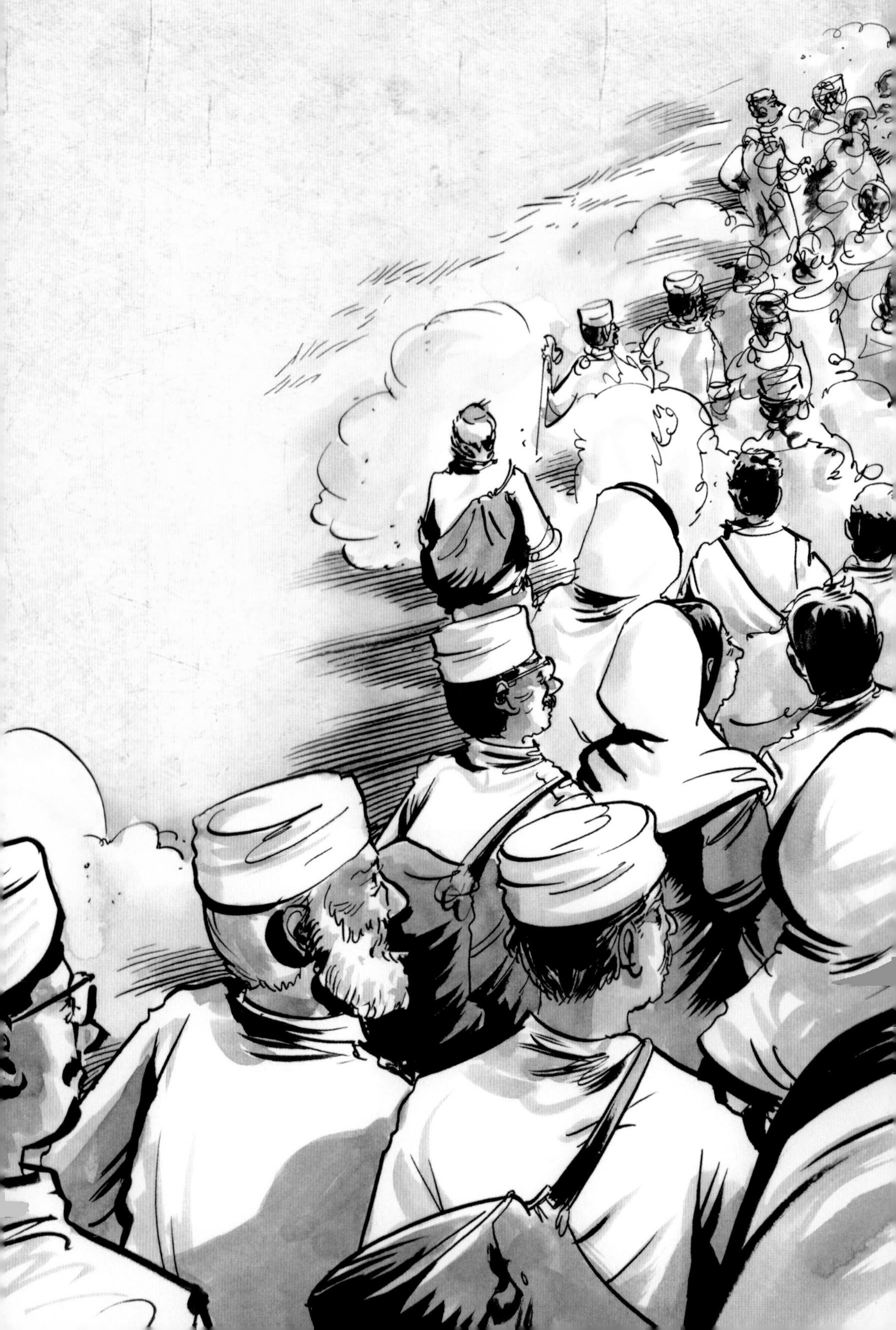

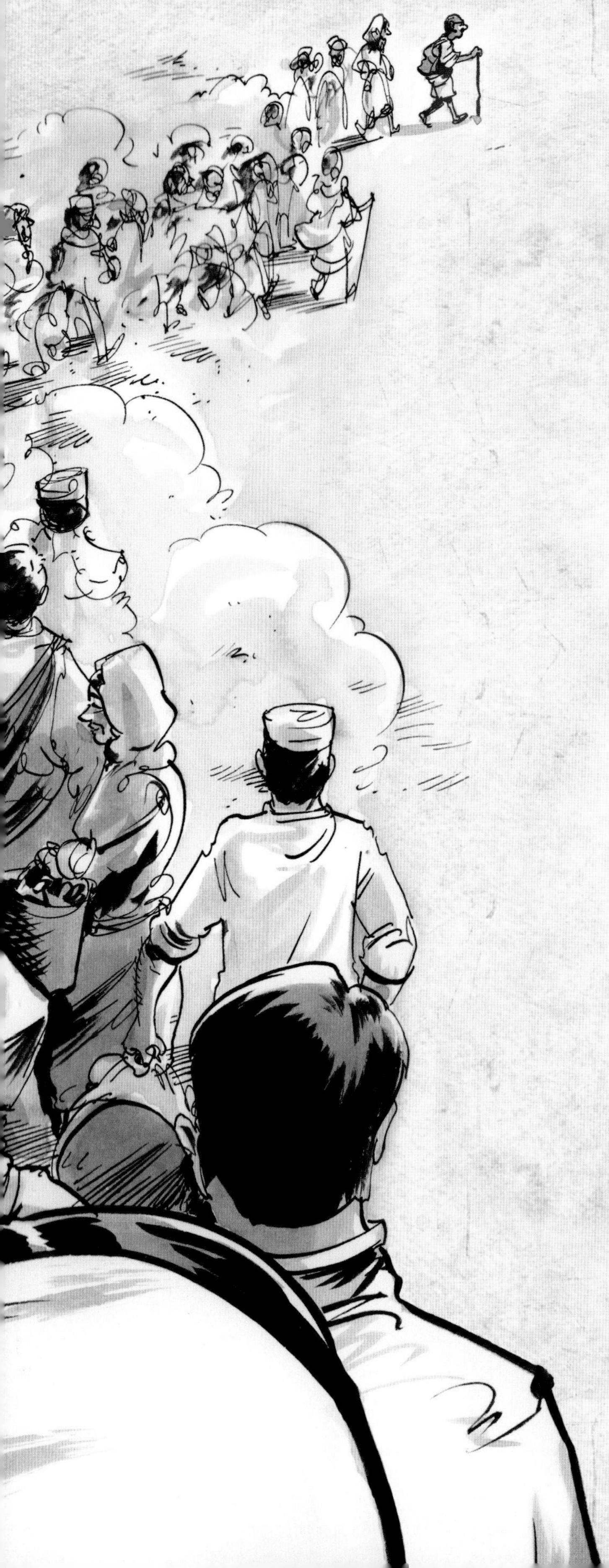

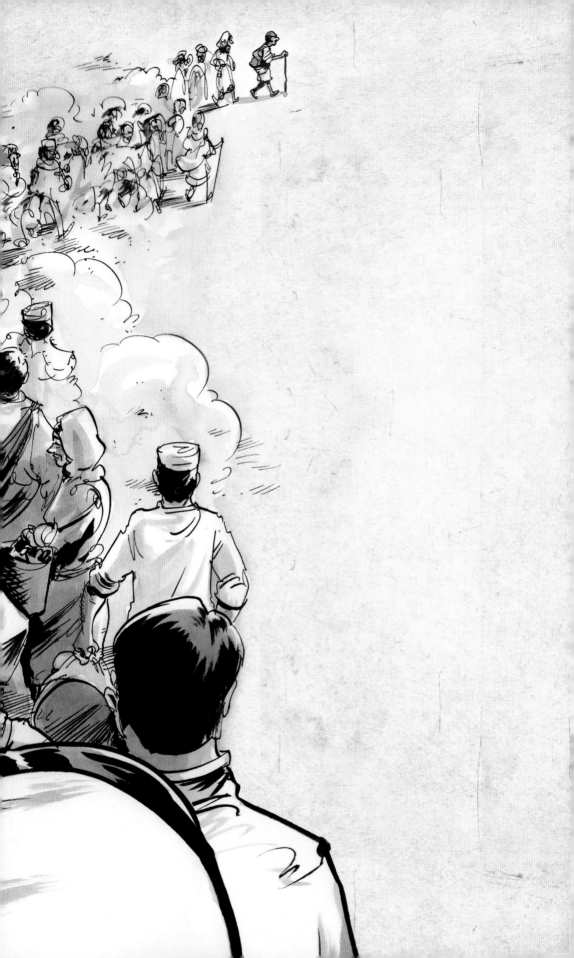

A GRAPHIC BIOGRAPHY
OF A HERO BY
BRAD MELTZER
ILLUSTRATED BY
ARTHUR ADAMS • JOHN CASSADAY
JIM CHEUNG • AMANDA CONNER
CARLOS D'ANDA • MICHAEL GAYDOS
GENE HA • STEPHANIE HANS
BRYAN HITCH • PHIL JIMENEZ
SIDDHARTH KOTIAN
DAVID LAFUENTE • DAVID MACK
ALEX MALEEV • FRANCIS MANAPUL
DAVID MARQUEZ • STEVE MCNIVEN
RAGS MORALES • SAUMIN PATEL
NATE POWELL • STEPHANE ROUX
MARCO RUDY • KAMOME SHIRAHAMA
BILL SIENKIEWICZ • ABHISHEK SINGH
Lettered by CHRISTOPHER ELIOPOULOS
Colored by ALEX SINCLAIR

ORDINARY PEOPLE CHANGE the WORLD

I AM Gandhi

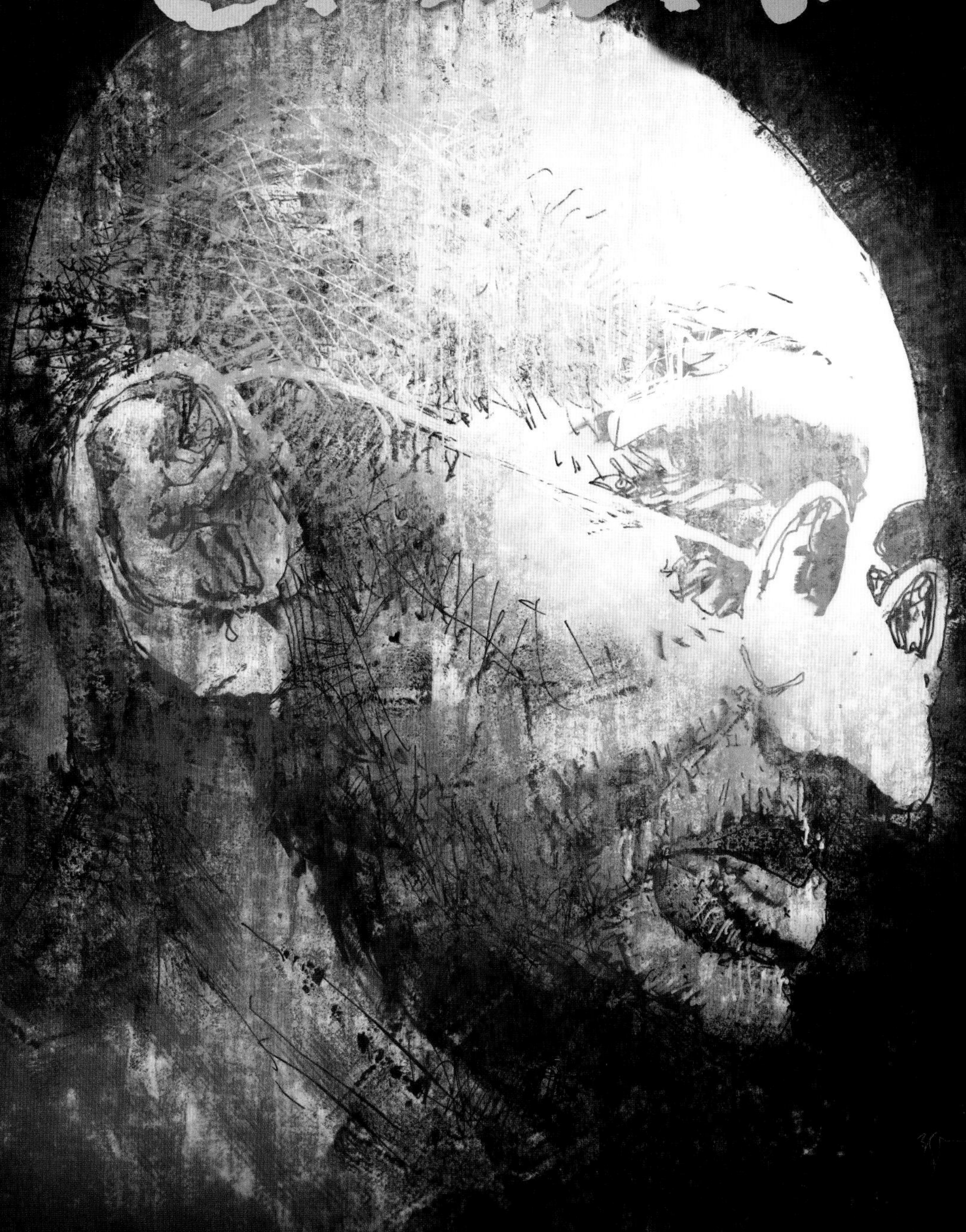

DIAL BOOKS

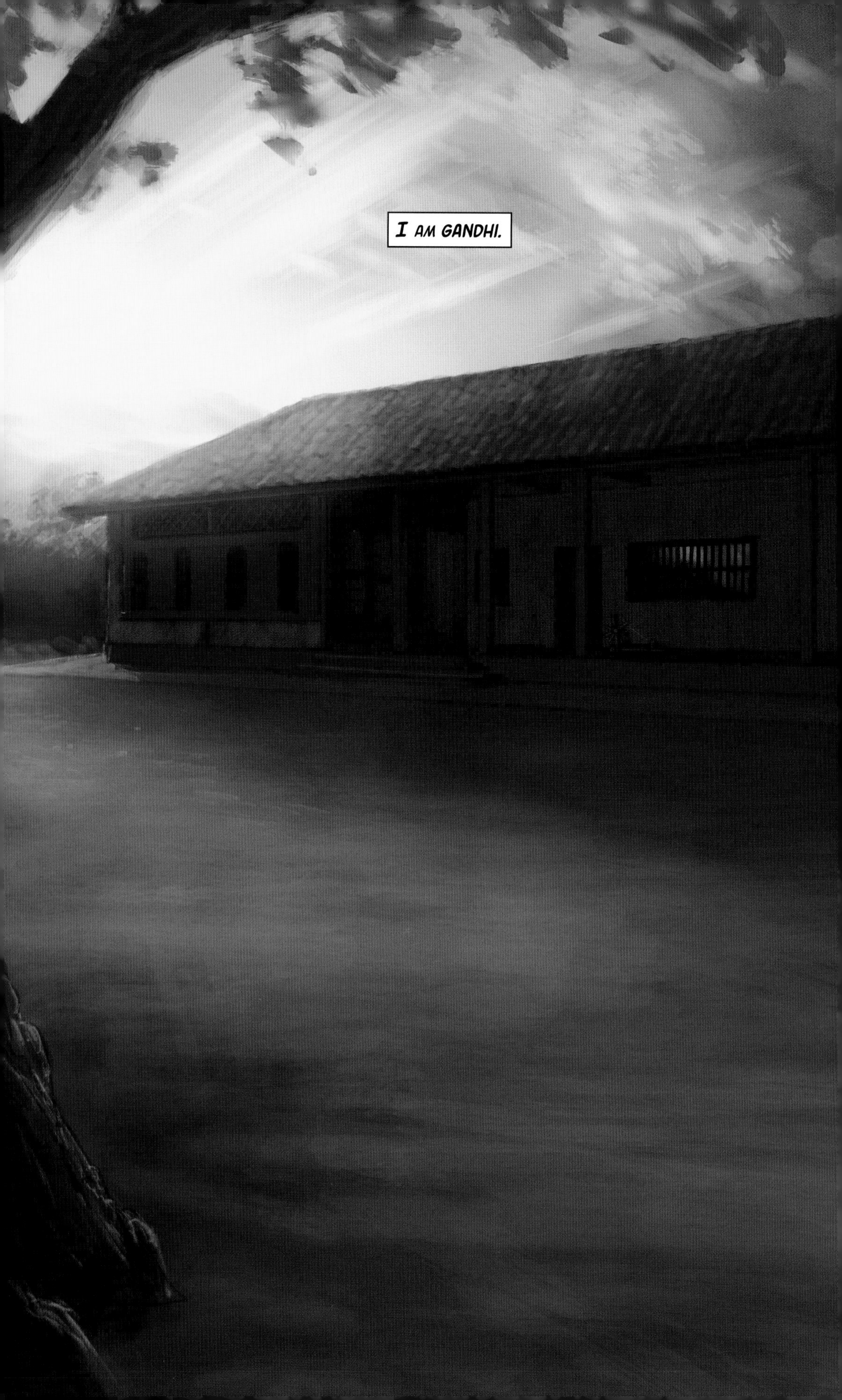
I AM GANDHI.

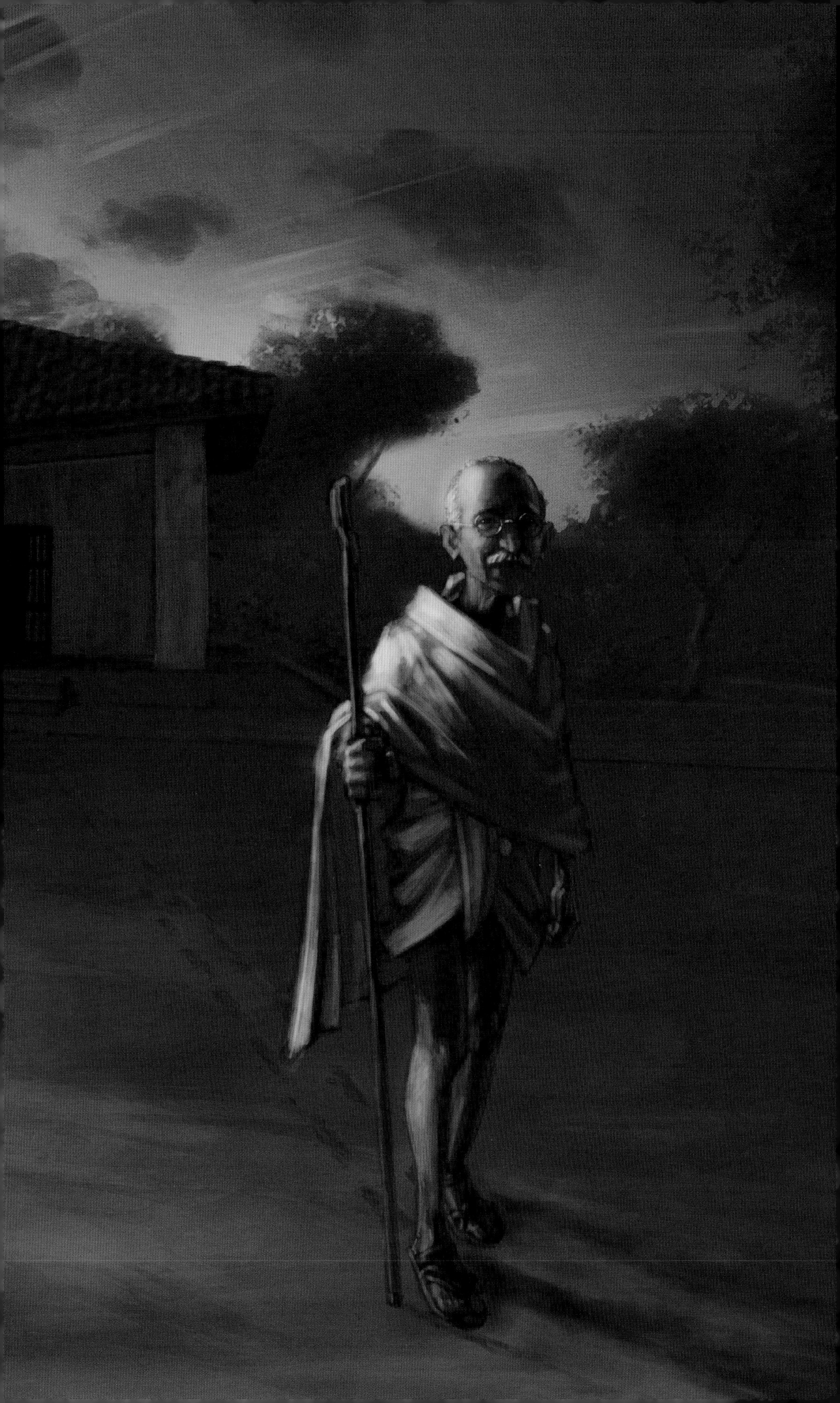

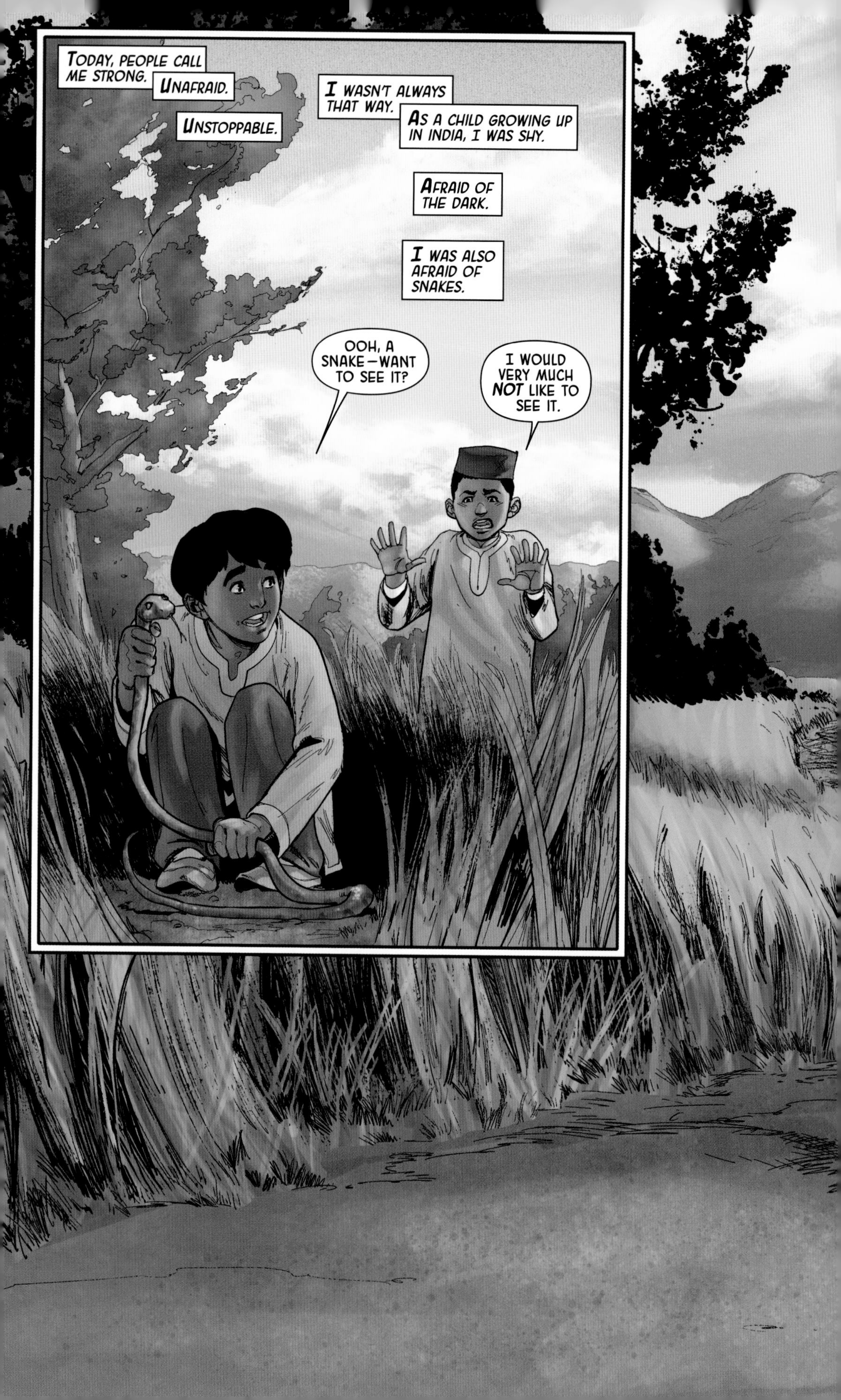

TODAY, PEOPLE CALL ME STRONG.
UNAFRAID.
UNSTOPPABLE.
I WASN'T ALWAYS THAT WAY.
AS A CHILD GROWING UP IN INDIA, I WAS SHY.
AFRAID OF THE DARK.
I WAS ALSO AFRAID OF SNAKES.
OOH, A SNAKE—WANT TO SEE IT?
I WOULD VERY MUCH NOT LIKE TO SEE IT.

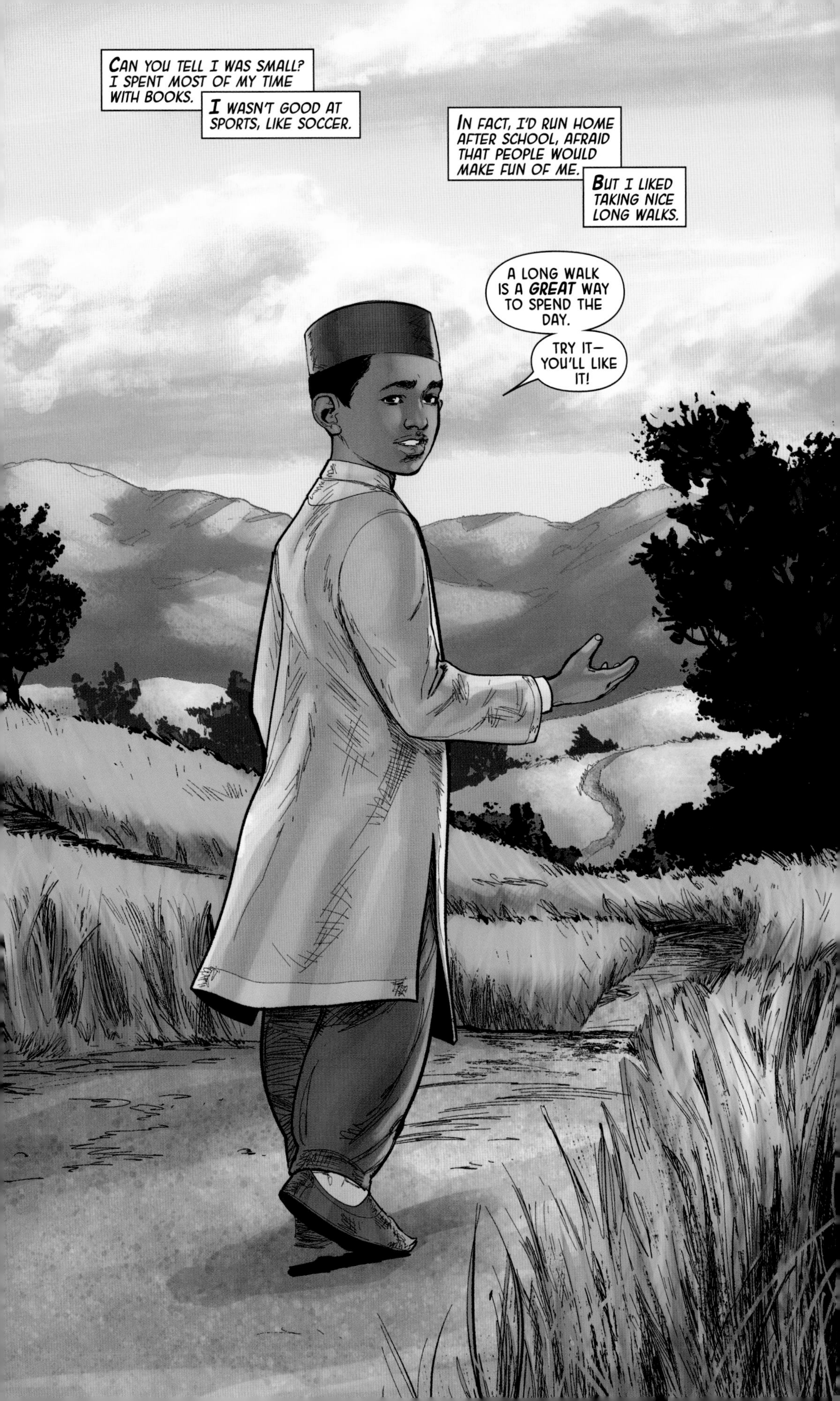

CAN YOU TELL I WAS SMALL? I SPENT MOST OF MY TIME WITH BOOKS.
I WASN'T GOOD AT SPORTS, LIKE SOCCER.
IN FACT, I'D RUN HOME AFTER SCHOOL, AFRAID THAT PEOPLE WOULD MAKE FUN OF ME.
BUT I LIKED TAKING NICE LONG WALKS.
A LONG WALK IS A GREAT WAY TO SPEND THE DAY.
TRY IT—YOU'LL LIKE IT!

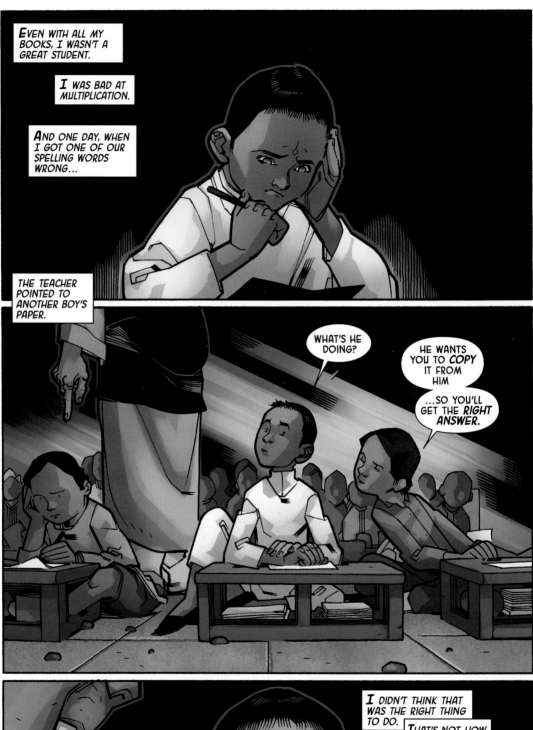

EVEN WITH ALL MY BOOKS, I WASN'T A GREAT STUDENT.

I WAS BAD AT MULTIPLICATION.

AND ONE DAY, WHEN I GOT ONE OF OUR SPELLING WORDS WRONG...

THE TEACHER POINTED TO ANOTHER BOY'S PAPER.

WHAT'S HE DOING?

HE WANTS YOU TO **COPY** IT FROM HIM

...SO YOU'LL GET THE **RIGHT** ANSWER.

I DIDN'T THINK THAT WAS THE RIGHT THING TO DO. **THAT'S** NOT HOW YOU LEARN.

WHEN THE TEACHER SCOLDED ME, I WASN'T BOTHERED. IN MY LIFE, I DID NOT COPY OTHERS' WORK.

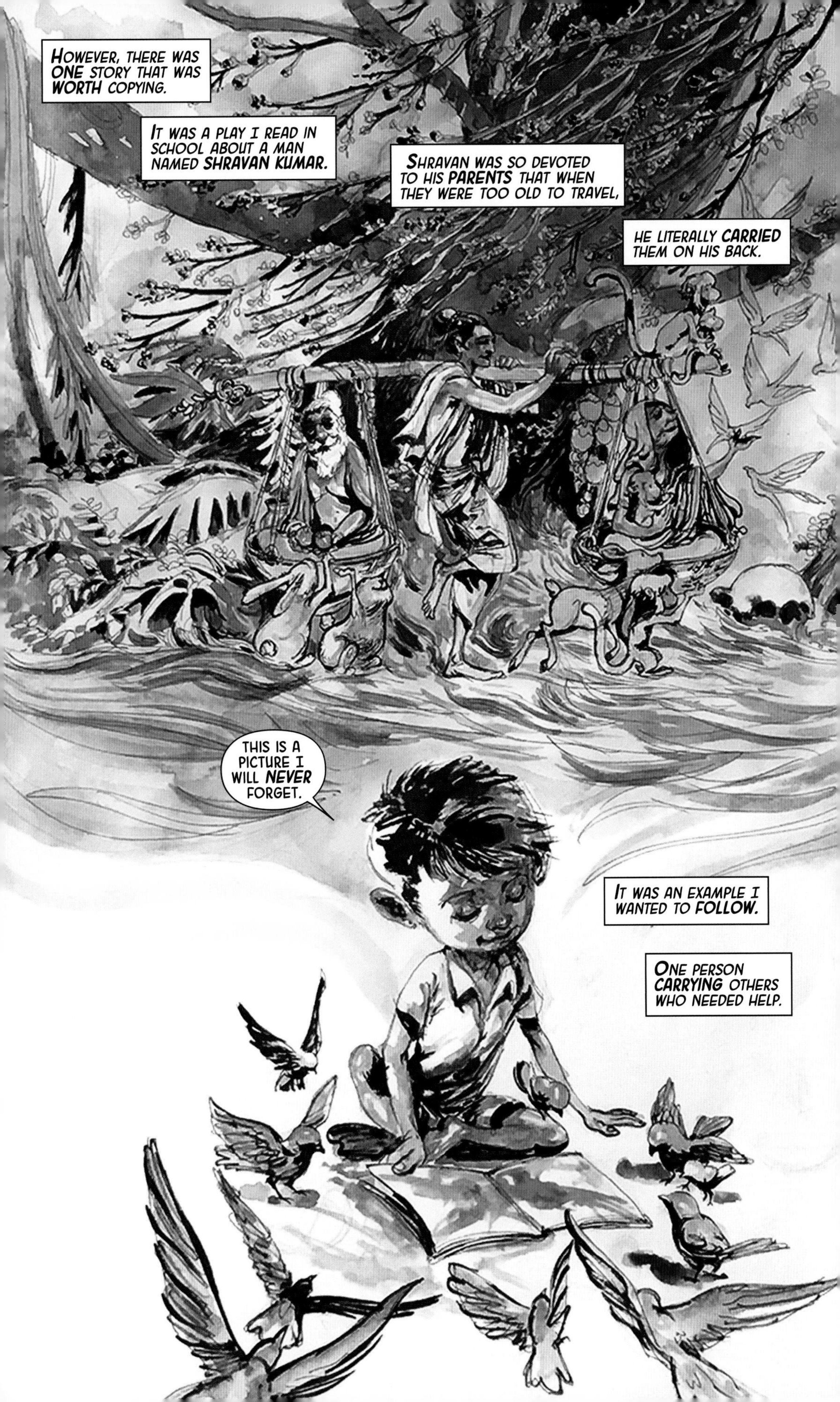

HOWEVER, THERE WAS ONE STORY THAT WAS WORTH COPYING.
IT WAS A PLAY I READ IN SCHOOL ABOUT A MAN NAMED SHRAVAN KUMAR.
SHRAVAN WAS SO DEVOTED TO HIS PARENTS THAT WHEN THEY WERE TOO OLD TO TRAVEL,
HE LITERALLY CARRIED THEM ON HIS BACK.
THIS IS A PICTURE I WILL NEVER FORGET.
IT WAS AN EXAMPLE I WANTED TO FOLLOW.
ONE PERSON CARRYING OTHERS WHO NEEDED HELP.

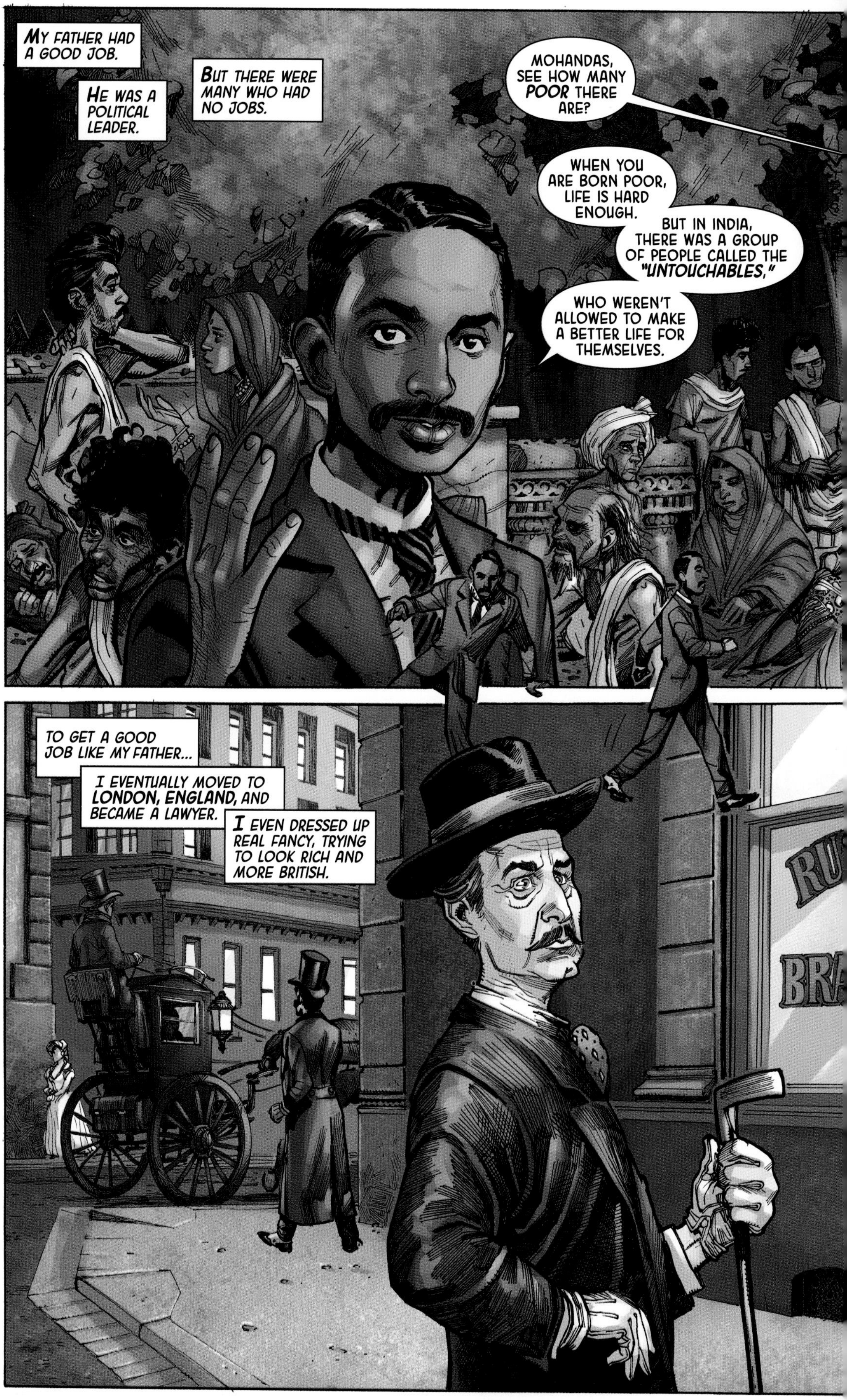
MY FATHER HAD A GOOD JOB.
HE WAS A POLITICAL LEADER.
BUT THERE WERE MANY WHO HAD NO JOBS.
MOHANDAS, SEE HOW MANY POOR THERE ARE?
WHEN YOU ARE BORN POOR, LIFE IS HARD ENOUGH.
BUT IN INDIA, THERE WAS A GROUP OF PEOPLE CALLED THE "UNTOUCHABLES,"
WHO WEREN'T ALLOWED TO MAKE A BETTER LIFE FOR THEMSELVES.
TO GET A GOOD JOB LIKE MY FATHER...
I EVENTUALLY MOVED TO LONDON, ENGLAND, AND BECAME A LAWYER.
I EVEN DRESSED UP REAL FANCY, TRYING TO LOOK RICH AND MORE BRITISH.

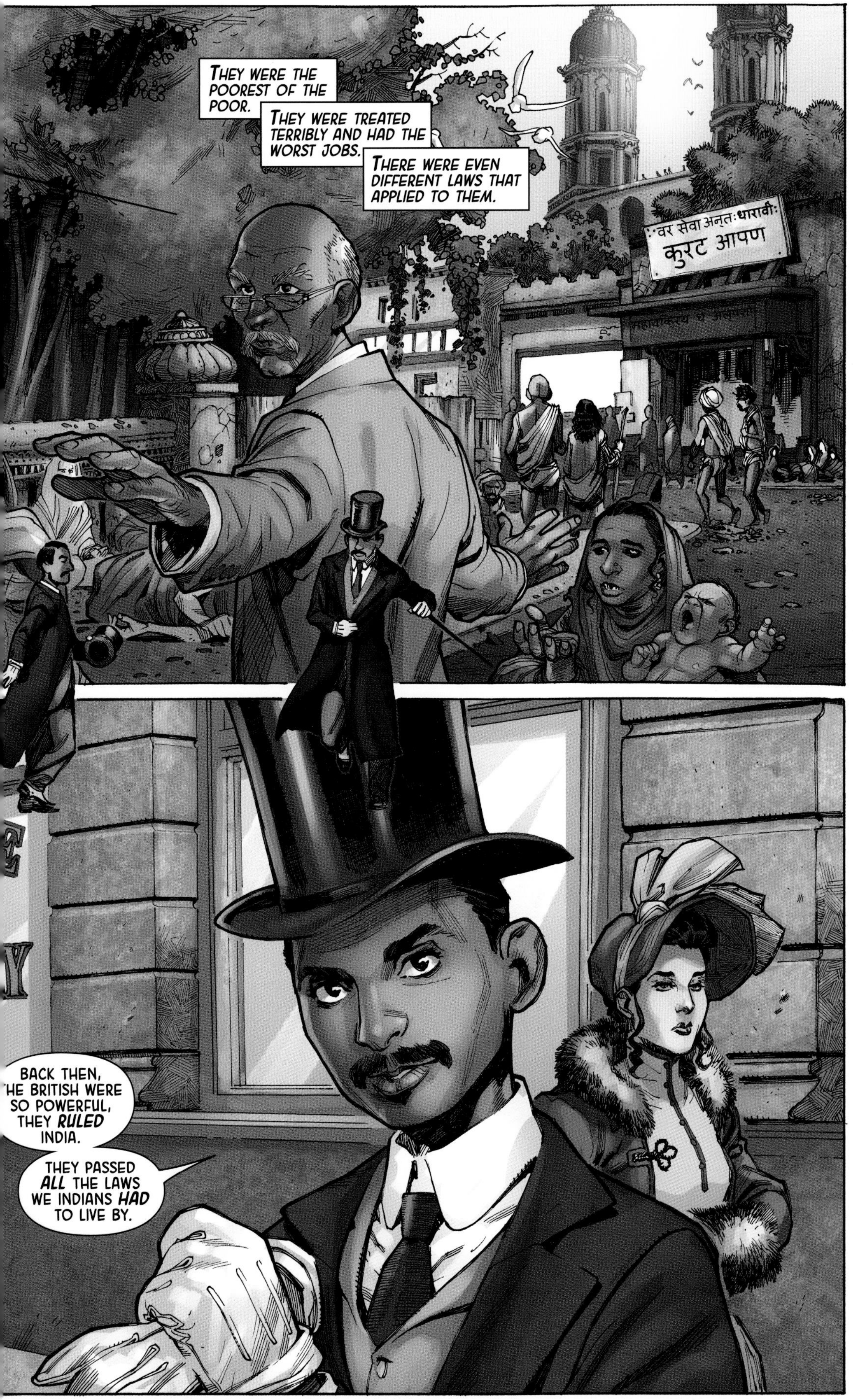

THEY WERE THE POOREST OF THE POOR.
THEY WERE TREATED TERRIBLY AND HAD THE WORST JOBS.
THERE WERE EVEN DIFFERENT LAWS THAT APPLIED TO THEM.
वर सेवा अन्तः धारावीः
कुरट आपण
BACK THEN, HE BRITISH WERE SO POWERFUL, THEY *RULED* INDIA.
THEY PASSED ***ALL*** THE LAWS WE INDIANS ***HAD*** TO LIVE BY.

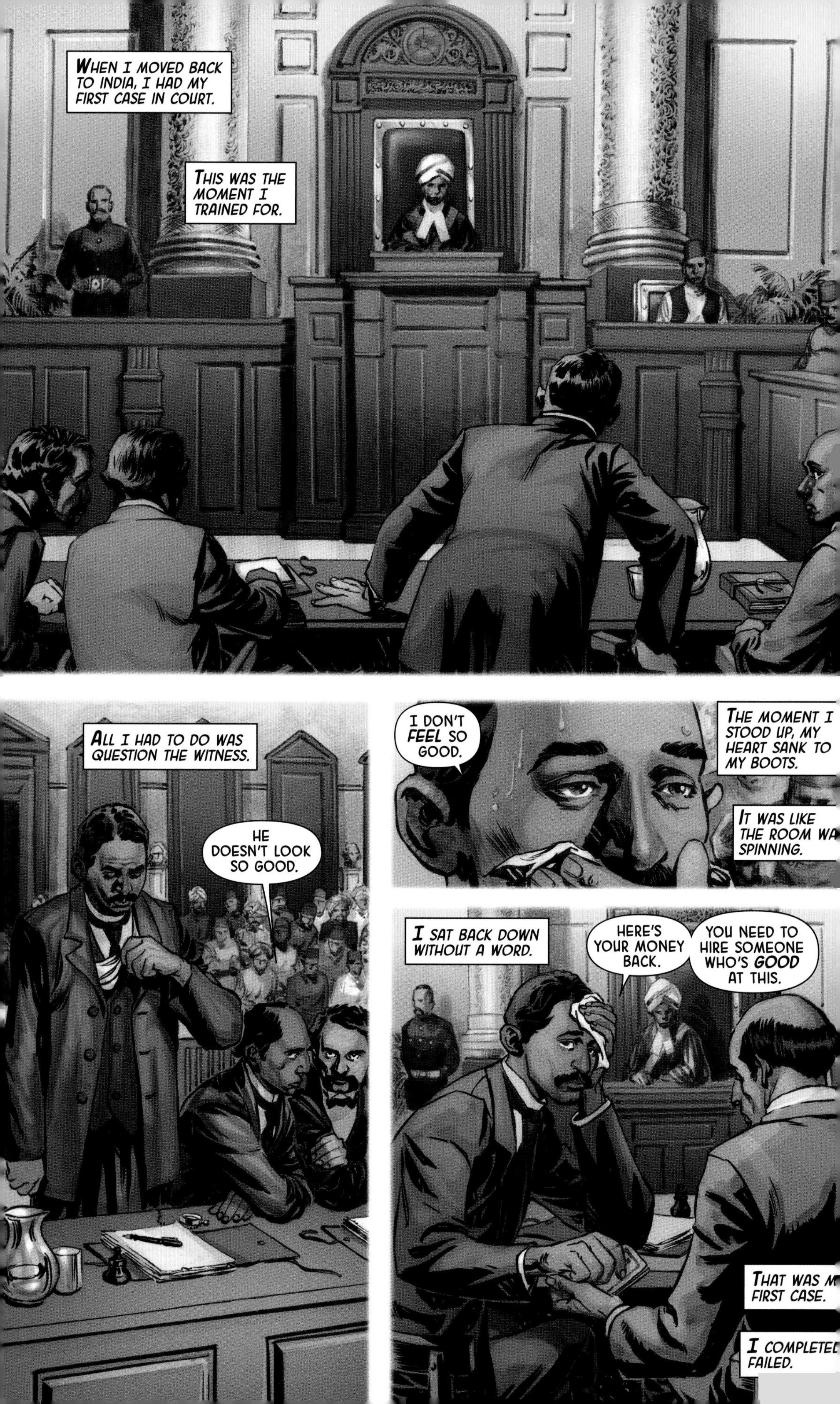
WHEN I MOVED BACK TO INDIA, I HAD MY FIRST CASE IN COURT.
THIS WAS THE MOMENT I TRAINED FOR.
ALL I HAD TO DO WAS QUESTION THE WITNESS.
HE DOESN'T LOOK SO GOOD.
I DON'T FEEL SO GOOD.
THE MOMENT I STOOD UP, MY HEART SANK TO MY BOOTS.
IT WAS LIKE THE ROOM WA
SPINNING.
I SAT BACK DOWN WITHOUT A WORD.
HERE'S YOUR MONEY BACK.
YOU NEED TO HIRE SOMEONE WHO'S GOOD AT THIS.
THAT WAS M
FIRST CASE.
I COMPLETE
FAILED.

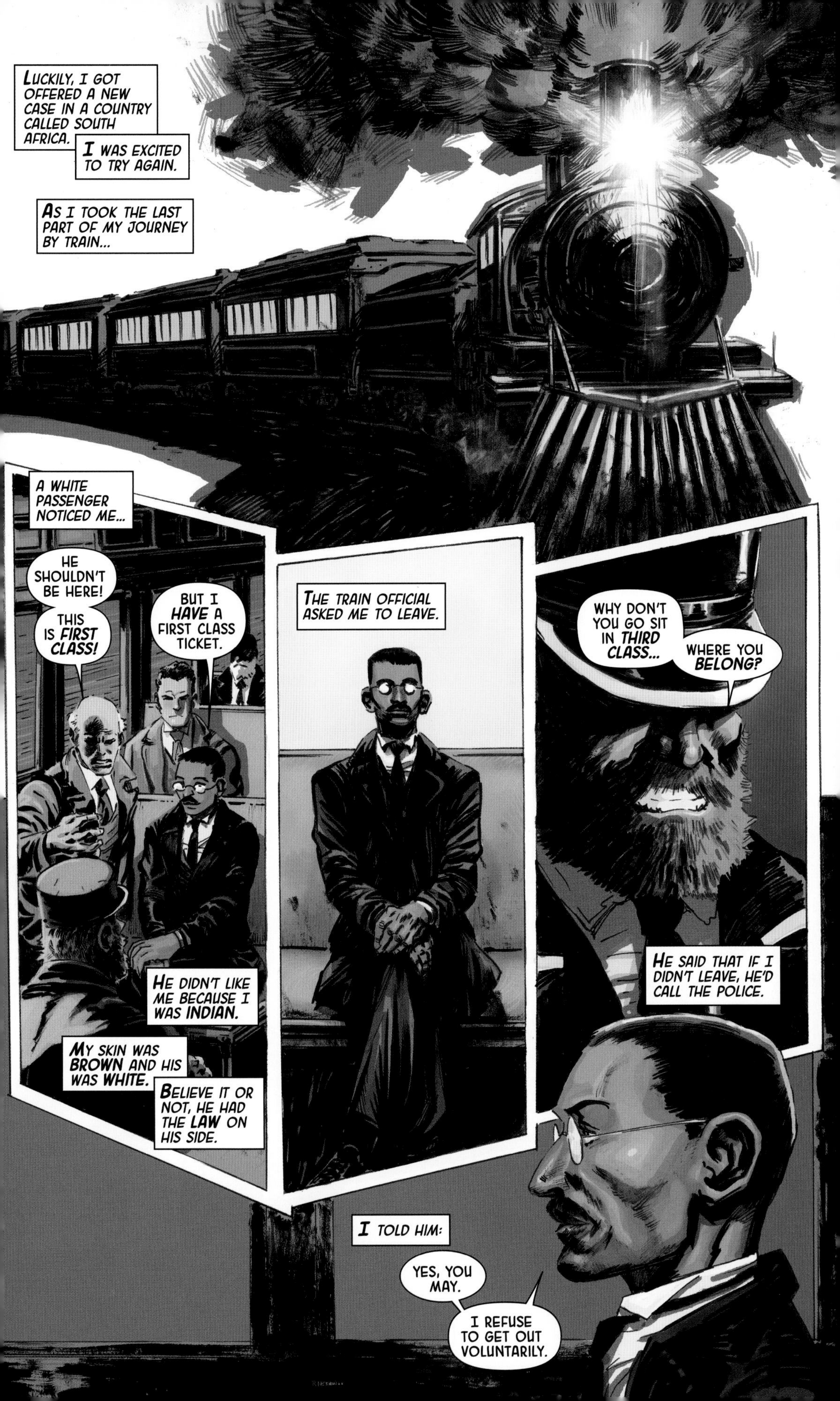

LUCKILY, I GOT OFFERED A NEW CASE IN A COUNTRY CALLED SOUTH AFRICA.
I WAS EXCITED TO TRY AGAIN.
AS I TOOK THE LAST PART OF MY JOURNEY BY TRAIN...
A WHITE PASSENGER NOTICED ME...
HE SHOULDN'T BE HERE!
THIS IS FIRST CLASS!
BUT I HAVE A FIRST CLASS TICKET.
HE DIDN'T LIKE ME BECAUSE I WAS INDIAN.
MY SKIN WAS BROWN AND HIS WAS WHITE.
BELIEVE IT OR NOT, HE HAD THE LAW ON HIS SIDE.
THE TRAIN OFFICIAL ASKED ME TO LEAVE.
WHY DON'T YOU GO SIT IN THIRD CLASS...
WHERE YOU BELONG?
HE SAID THAT IF I DIDN'T LEAVE, HE'D CALL THE POLICE.
I TOLD HIM:
YES, YOU MAY.
I REFUSE TO GET OUT VOLUNTARILY.

A POLICEMAN **PUSHED** ME OUT OF THE TRAIN AND TOSSED MY STUFF ONTO THE STATION PLATFORM.

GOOD RIDDANCE!

IT WAS **COLD** IN THAT STATION. **AND DARK.**

I COULD'VE GOTTEN **BACK** ON THE TRAIN AND SAT IN **THIRD CLASS.**

INSTEAD, I STAYED THERE **ALL NIGHT.**

SHIVERING.

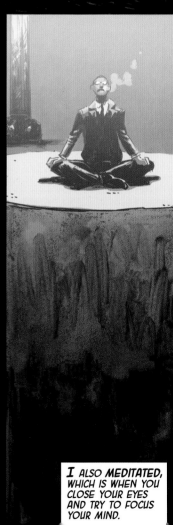

I ALSO MEDITATED, WHICH IS WHEN YOU CLOSE YOUR EYES AND TRY TO FOCUS YOUR MIND.

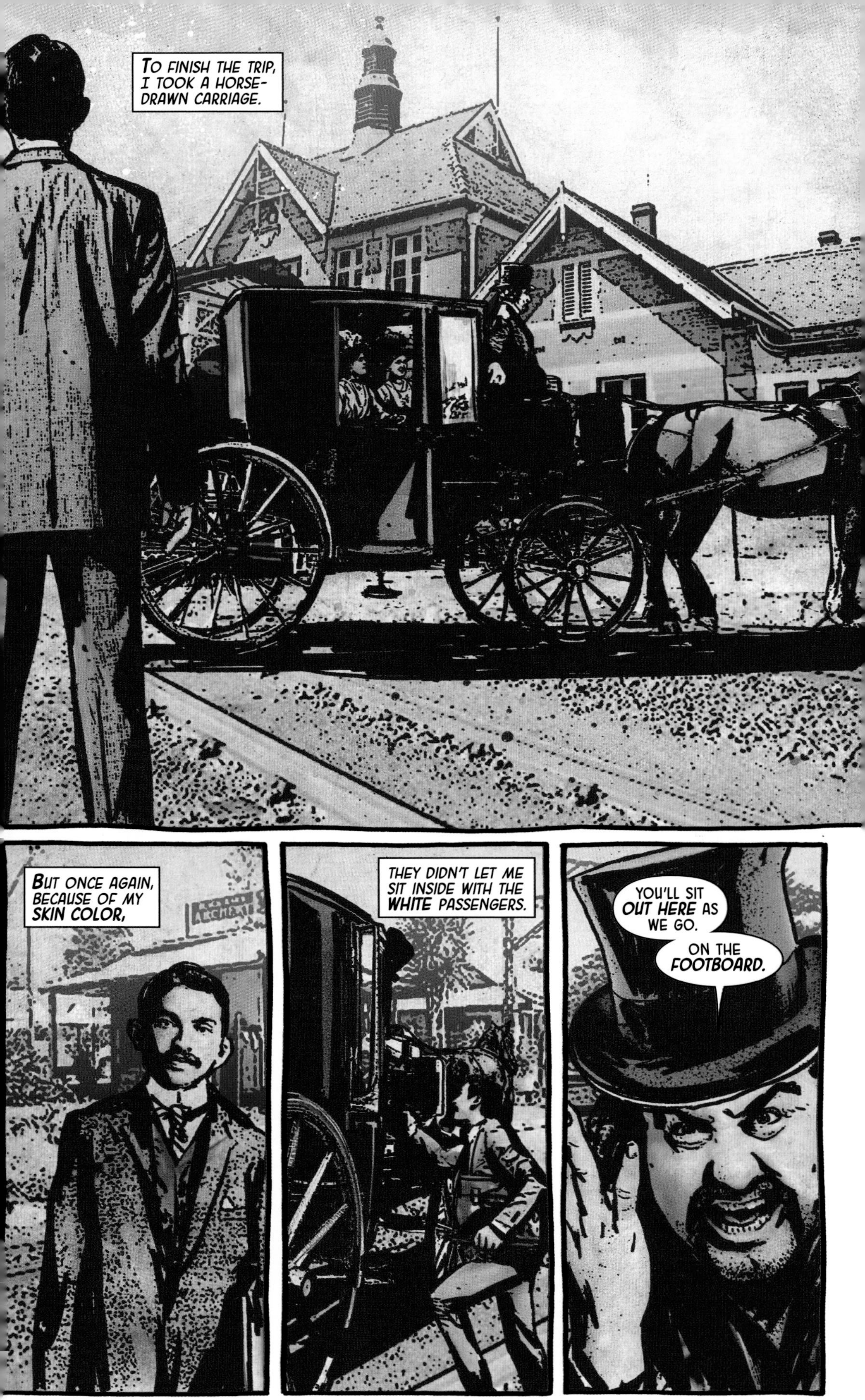

TO FINISH THE TRIP, I TOOK A HORSE-DRAWN CARRIAGE.
BUT ONCE AGAIN, BECAUSE OF MY SKIN COLOR,
THEY DIDN'T LET ME SIT INSIDE WITH THE WHITE PASSENGERS.
YOU'LL SIT OUT HERE AS WE GO.
ON THE FOOTBOARD.

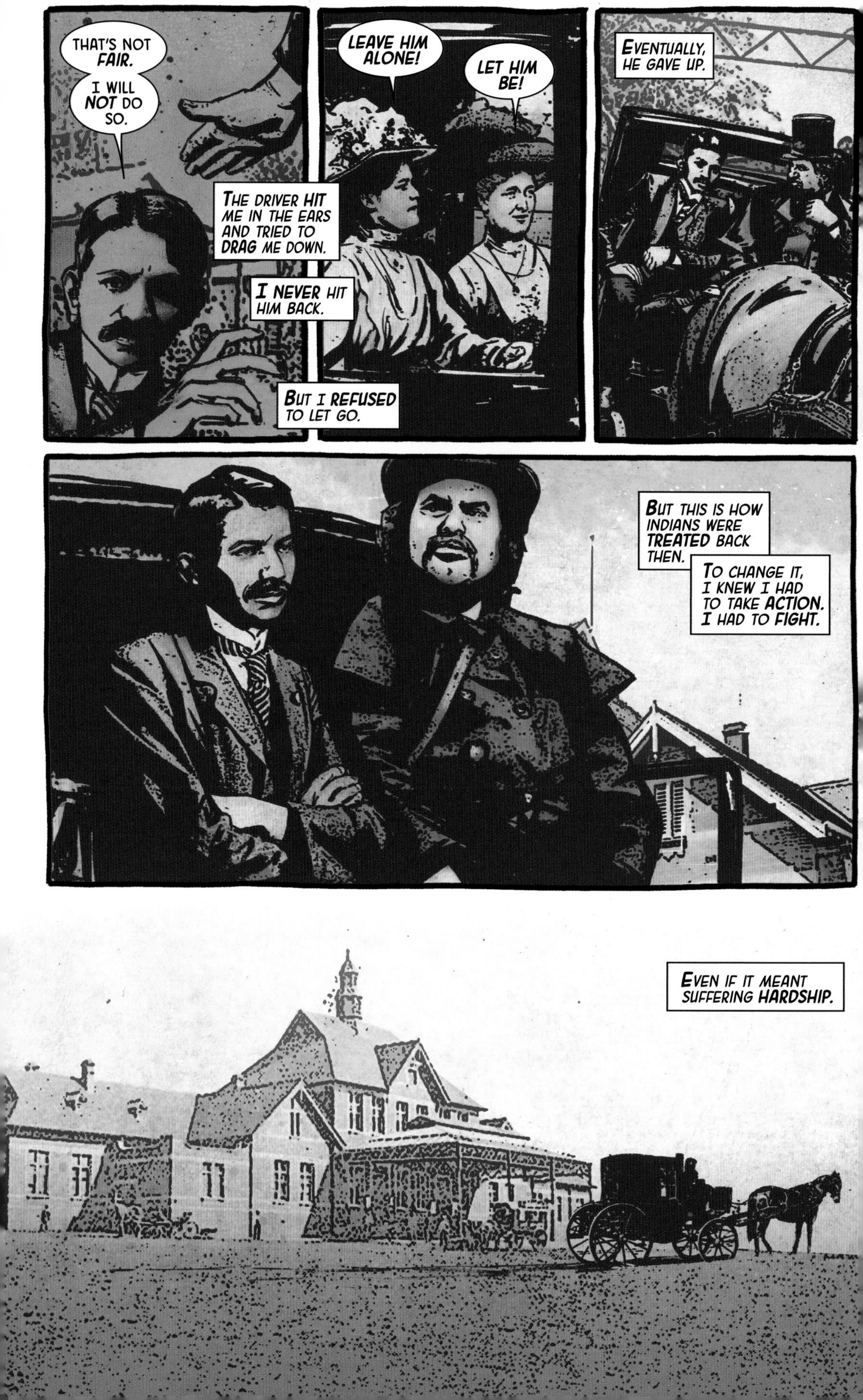
THAT'S NOT FAIR.
I WILL NOT DO SO.
THE DRIVER HIT ME IN THE EARS AND TRIED TO DRAG ME DOWN.
I NEVER HIT HIM BACK.
LEAVE HIM ALONE!
LET HIM BE!
BUT I REFUSED TO LET GO.
EVENTUALLY, HE GAVE UP.
BUT THIS IS HOW INDIANS WERE TREATED BACK THEN.
TO CHANGE IT, I KNEW I HAD TO TAKE ACTION. I HAD TO FIGHT.
EVEN IF IT MEANT SUFFERING HARDSHIP.

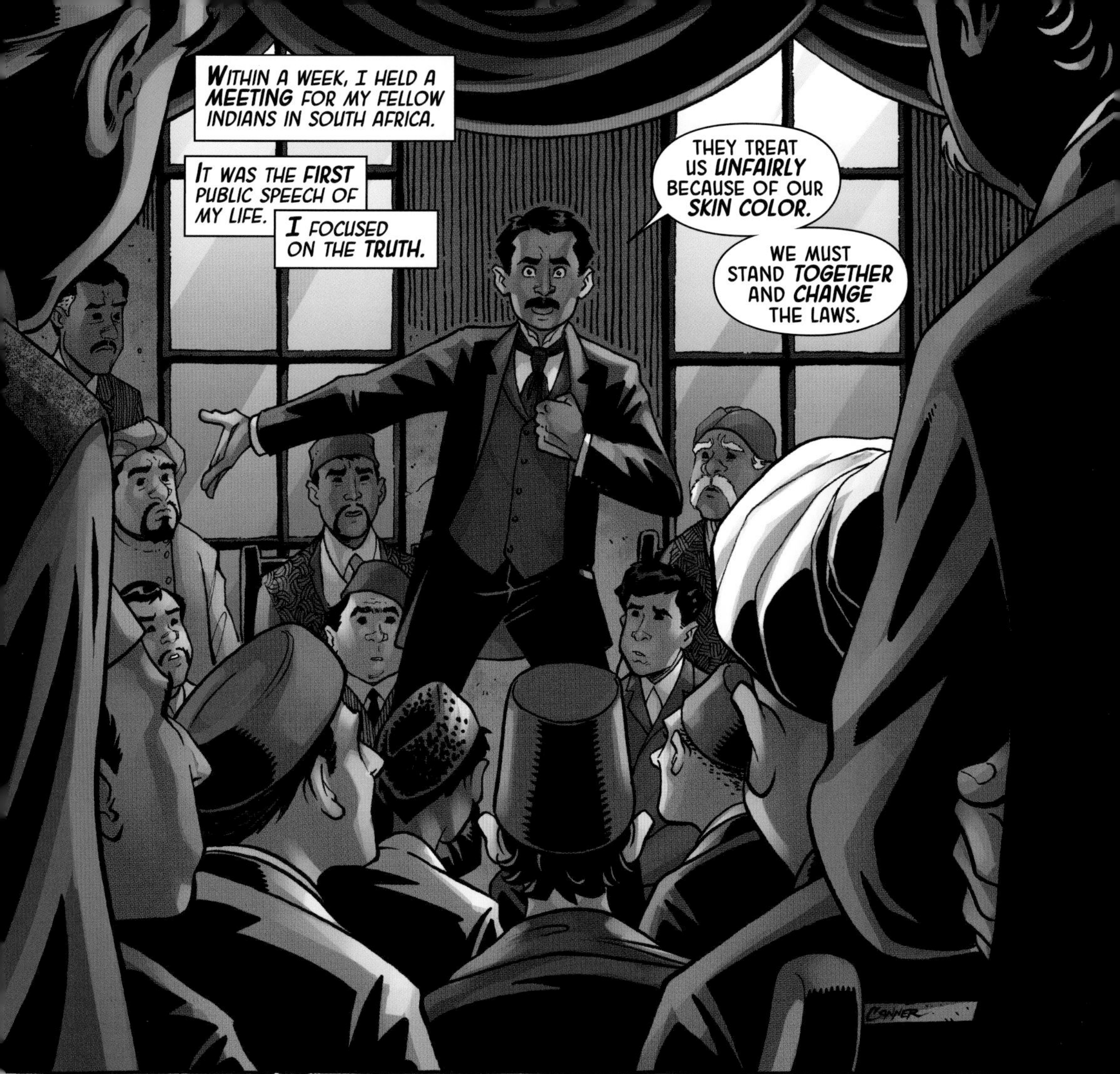

WITHIN A WEEK, I HELD A MEETING FOR MY FELLOW INDIANS IN SOUTH AFRICA.
IT WAS THE FIRST PUBLIC SPEECH OF MY LIFE.
I FOCUSED ON THE TRUTH.
THEY TREAT US UNFAIRLY BECAUSE OF OUR SKIN COLOR.
WE MUST STAND TOGETHER AND CHANGE THE LAWS.

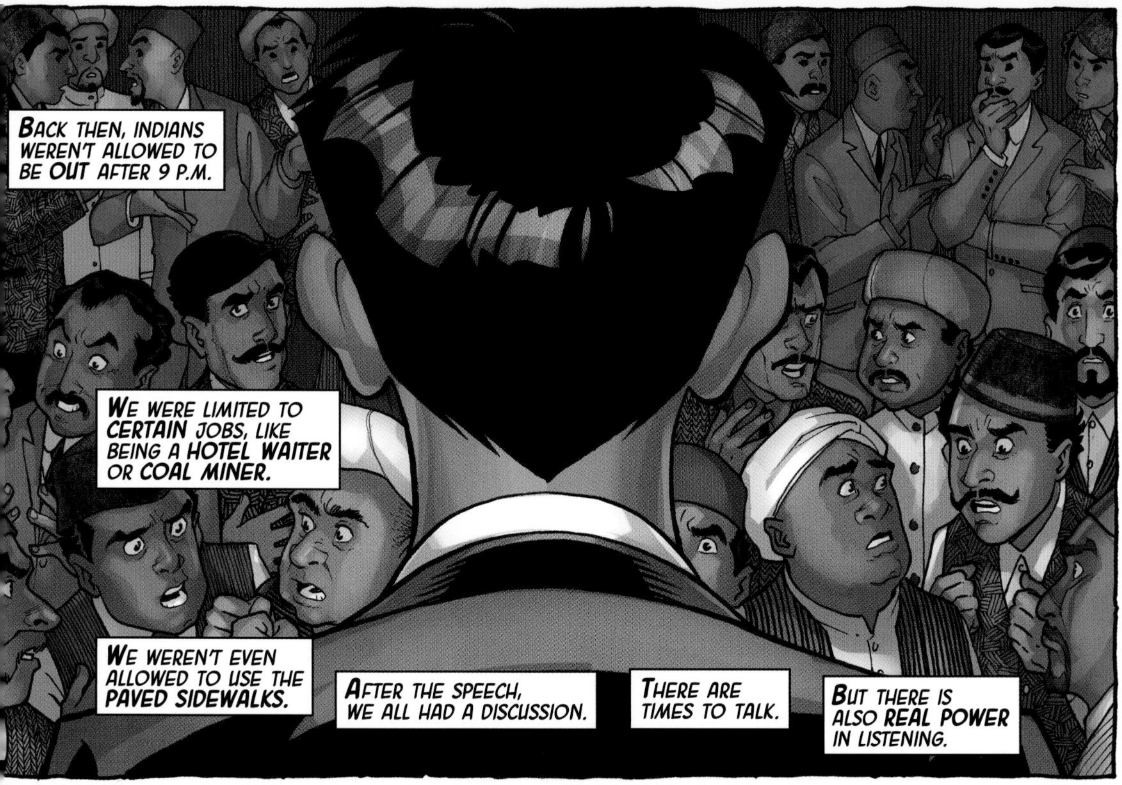

BACK THEN, INDIANS WEREN'T ALLOWED TO BE OUT AFTER 9 P.M.
WE WERE LIMITED TO CERTAIN JOBS, LIKE BEING A HOTEL WAITER OR COAL MINER.
WE WEREN'T EVEN ALLOWED TO USE THE PAVED SIDEWALKS.
AFTER THE SPEECH, WE ALL HAD A DISCUSSION.
THERE ARE TIMES TO TALK.
BUT THERE IS ALSO REAL POWER IN LISTENING.

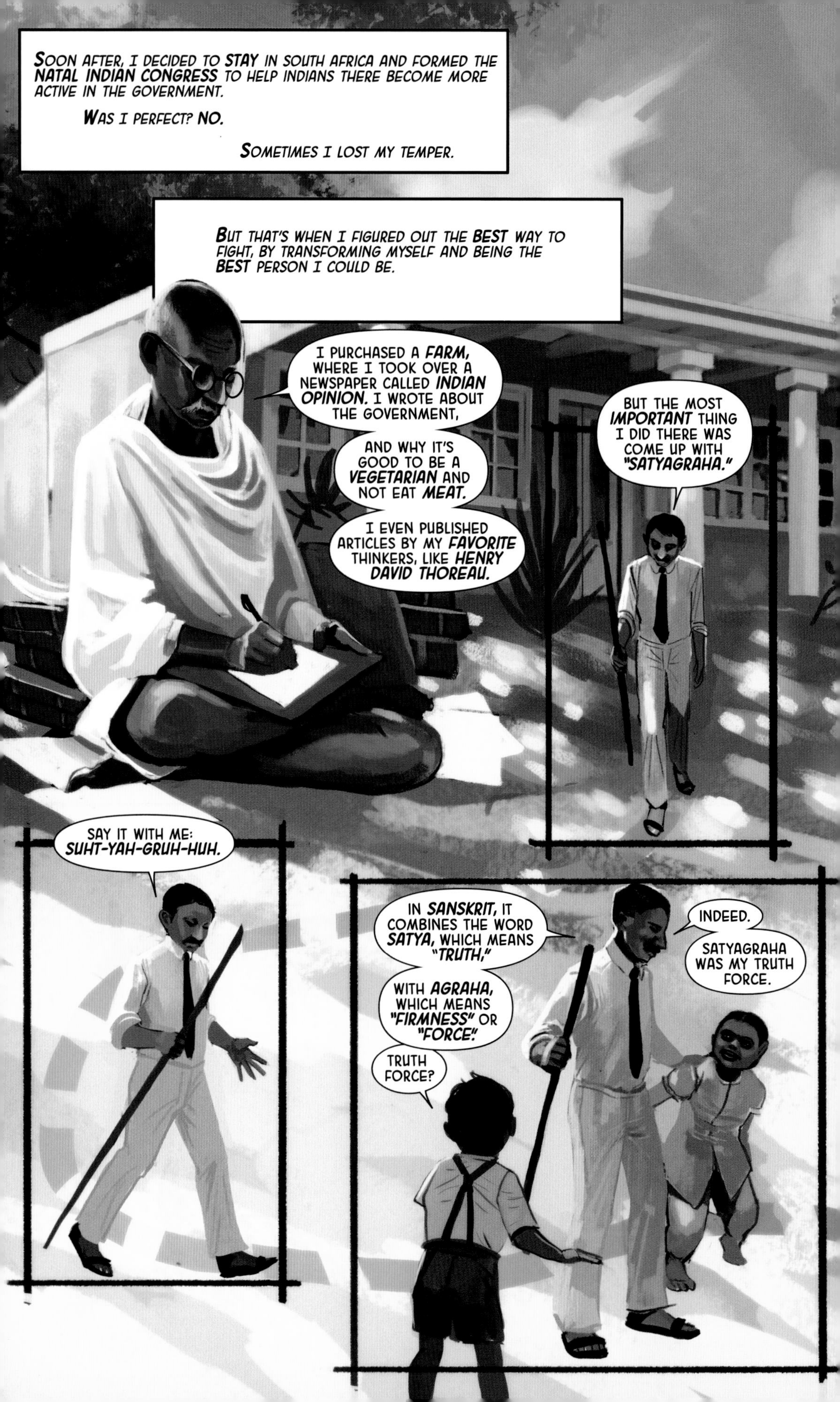
SOON AFTER, I DECIDED TO STAY IN SOUTH AFRICA AND FORMED THE NATAL INDIAN CONGRESS TO HELP INDIANS THERE BECOME MORE ACTIVE IN THE GOVERNMENT.
WAS I PERFECT? NO.
SOMETIMES I LOST MY TEMPER.
BUT THAT'S WHEN I FIGURED OUT THE BEST WAY TO FIGHT, BY TRANSFORMING MYSELF AND BEING THE BEST PERSON I COULD BE.
I PURCHASED A FARM, WHERE I TOOK OVER A NEWSPAPER CALLED INDIAN OPINION. I WROTE ABOUT THE GOVERNMENT,
AND WHY IT'S GOOD TO BE A VEGETARIAN AND NOT EAT MEAT.
I EVEN PUBLISHED ARTICLES BY MY FAVORITE THINKERS, LIKE HENRY DAVID THOREAU.
BUT THE MOST IMPORTANT THING I DID THERE WAS COME UP WITH "SATYAGRAHA."
SAY IT WITH ME: SUHT-YAH-GRUH-HUH.
IN SANSKRIT, IT COMBINES THE WORD SATYA, WHICH MEANS "TRUTH,"
WITH AGRAHA, WHICH MEANS "FIRMNESS" OR "FORCE."
TRUTH FORCE?
INDEED.
SATYAGRAHA WAS MY TRUTH FORCE.

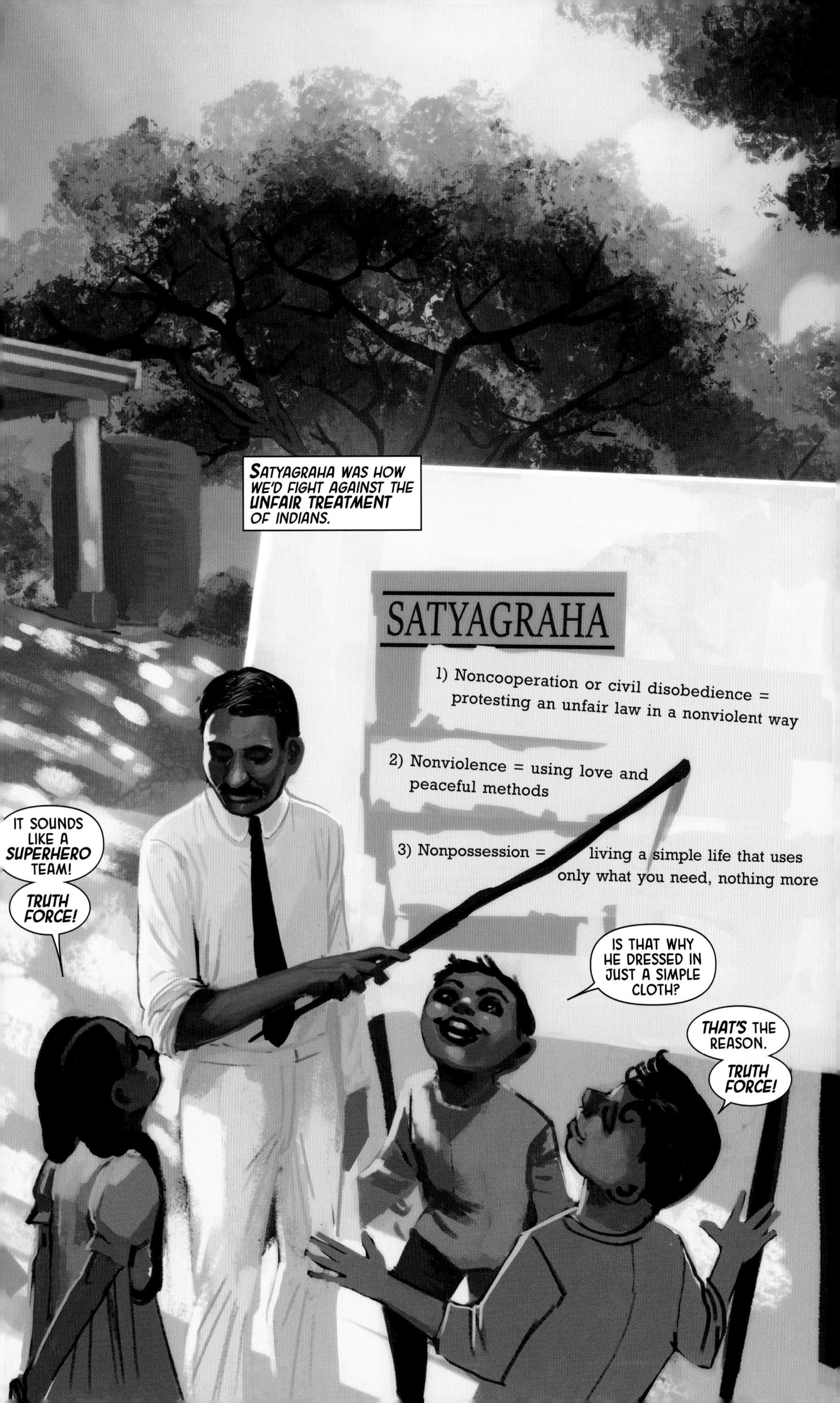
SATYAGRAHA WAS HOW WE'D FIGHT AGAINST THE UNFAIR TREATMENT OF INDIANS.
SATYAGRAHA
1) Noncooperation or civil disobedience = protesting an unfair law in a nonviolent way
2) Nonviolence = using love and peaceful methods
3) Nonpossession = living a simple life that uses only what you need, nothing more
IT SOUNDS LIKE A SUPERHERO TEAM!
TRUTH FORCE!
IS THAT WHY HE DRESSED IN JUST A SIMPLE CLOTH?
THAT'S THE REASON.
TRUTH FORCE!

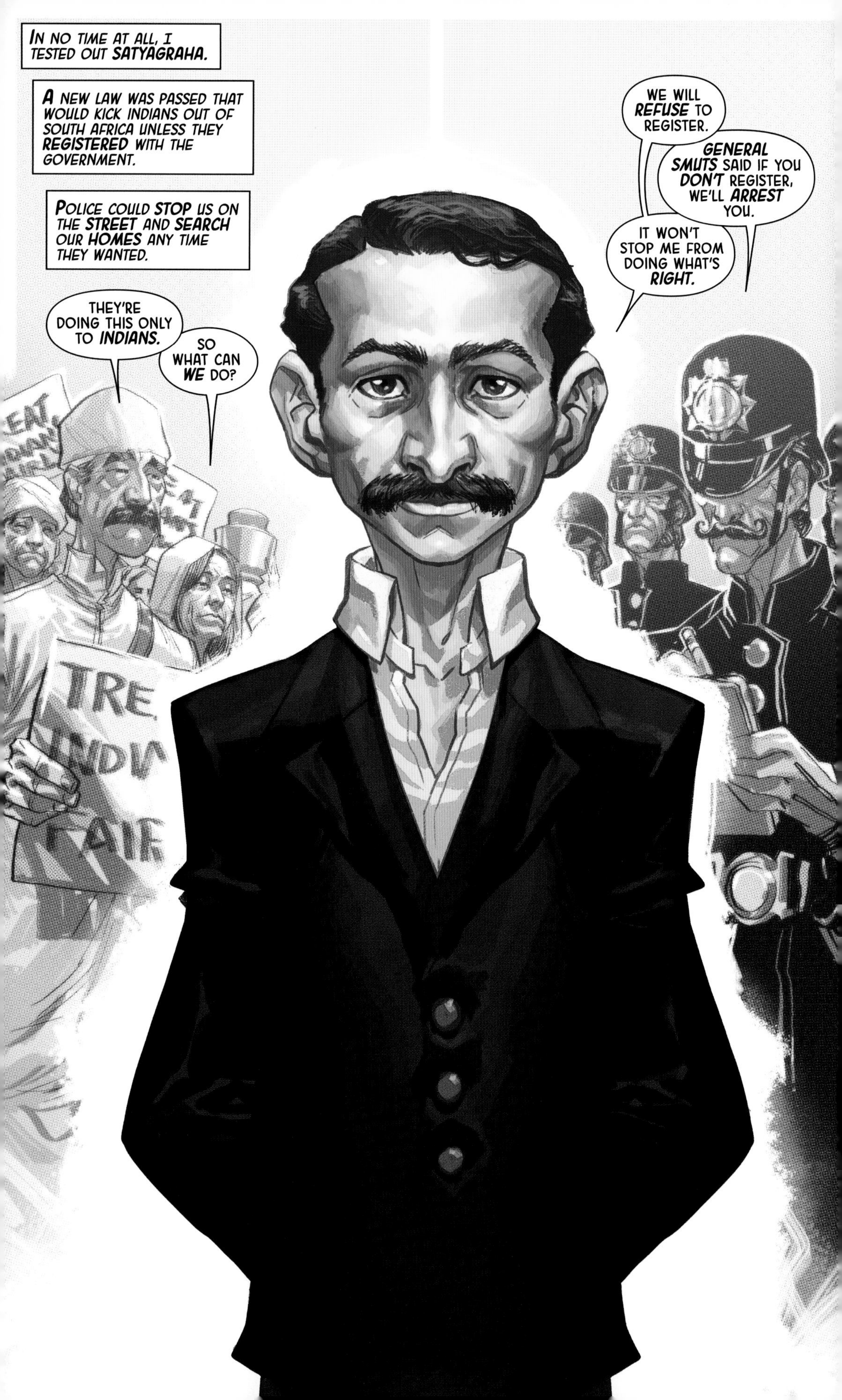

IN NO TIME AT ALL, I TESTED OUT SATYAGRAHA.
A NEW LAW WAS PASSED THAT WOULD KICK INDIANS OUT OF SOUTH AFRICA UNLESS THEY REGISTERED WITH THE GOVERNMENT.
POLICE COULD STOP US ON THE STREET AND SEARCH OUR HOMES ANY TIME THEY WANTED.
THEY'RE DOING THIS ONLY TO INDIANS.
SO WHAT CAN WE DO?
WE WILL REFUSE TO REGISTER.
GENERAL SMUTS SAID IF YOU DON'T REGISTER, WE'LL ARREST YOU.
IT WON'T STOP ME FROM DOING WHAT'S RIGHT.

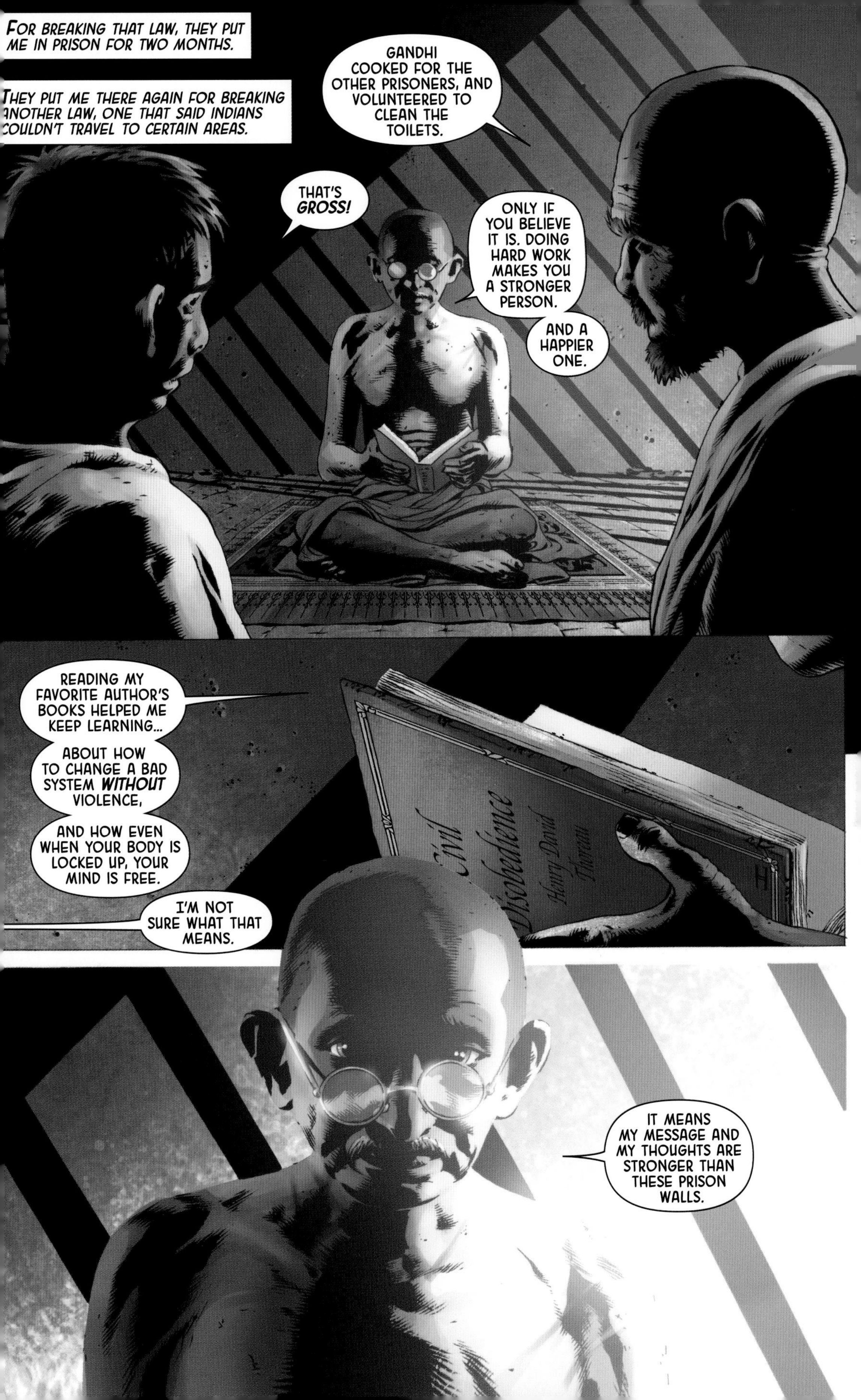
FOR BREAKING THAT LAW, THEY PUT ME IN PRISON FOR TWO MONTHS.
THEY PUT ME THERE AGAIN FOR BREAKING ANOTHER LAW, ONE THAT SAID INDIANS COULDN'T TRAVEL TO CERTAIN AREAS.
GANDHI COOKED FOR THE OTHER PRISONERS, AND VOLUNTEERED TO CLEAN THE TOILETS.
THAT'S *GROSS!*
ONLY IF YOU BELIEVE IT IS. DOING HARD WORK MAKES YOU A STRONGER PERSON.
AND A HAPPIER ONE.
READING MY FAVORITE AUTHOR'S BOOKS HELPED ME KEEP LEARNING...
ABOUT HOW TO CHANGE A BAD SYSTEM ***WITHOUT*** VIOLENCE,
AND HOW EVEN WHEN YOUR BODY IS LOCKED UP, YOUR MIND IS FREE.
Disobedience
Henry David
Thoreau
I'M NOT SURE WHAT THAT MEANS.
IT MEANS MY MESSAGE AND MY THOUGHTS ARE STRONGER THAN THESE PRISON WALLS.

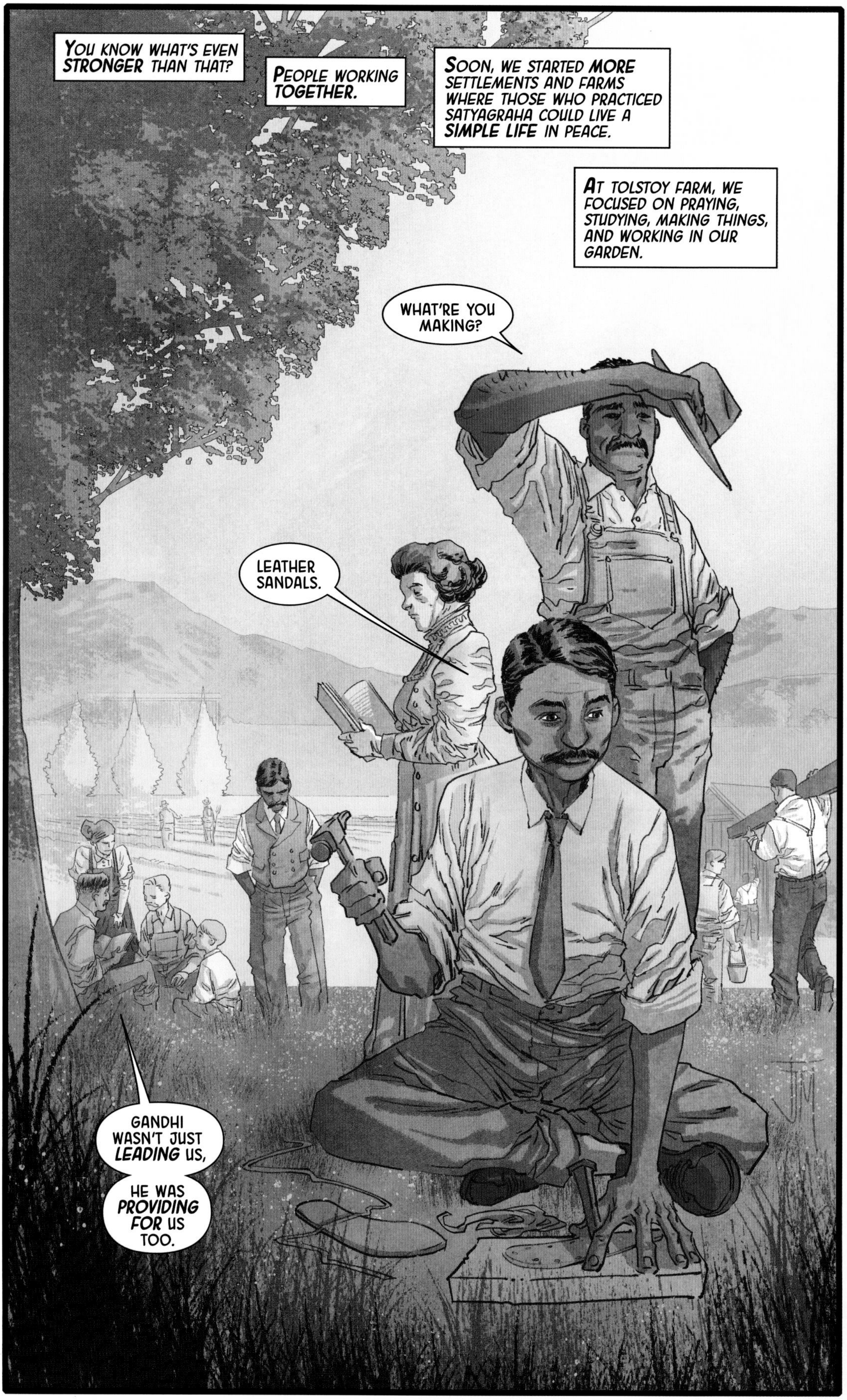
You know what's even STRONGER than that?
People working TOGETHER.
Soon, we started MORE settlements and farms where those who practiced Satyagraha could live a SIMPLE LIFE in peace.
At Tolstoy Farm, we focused on praying, studying, making things, and working in our garden.
WHAT'RE YOU MAKING?
LEATHER SANDALS.
GANDHI WASN'T JUST LEADING US,
HE WAS PROVIDING FOR US TOO.

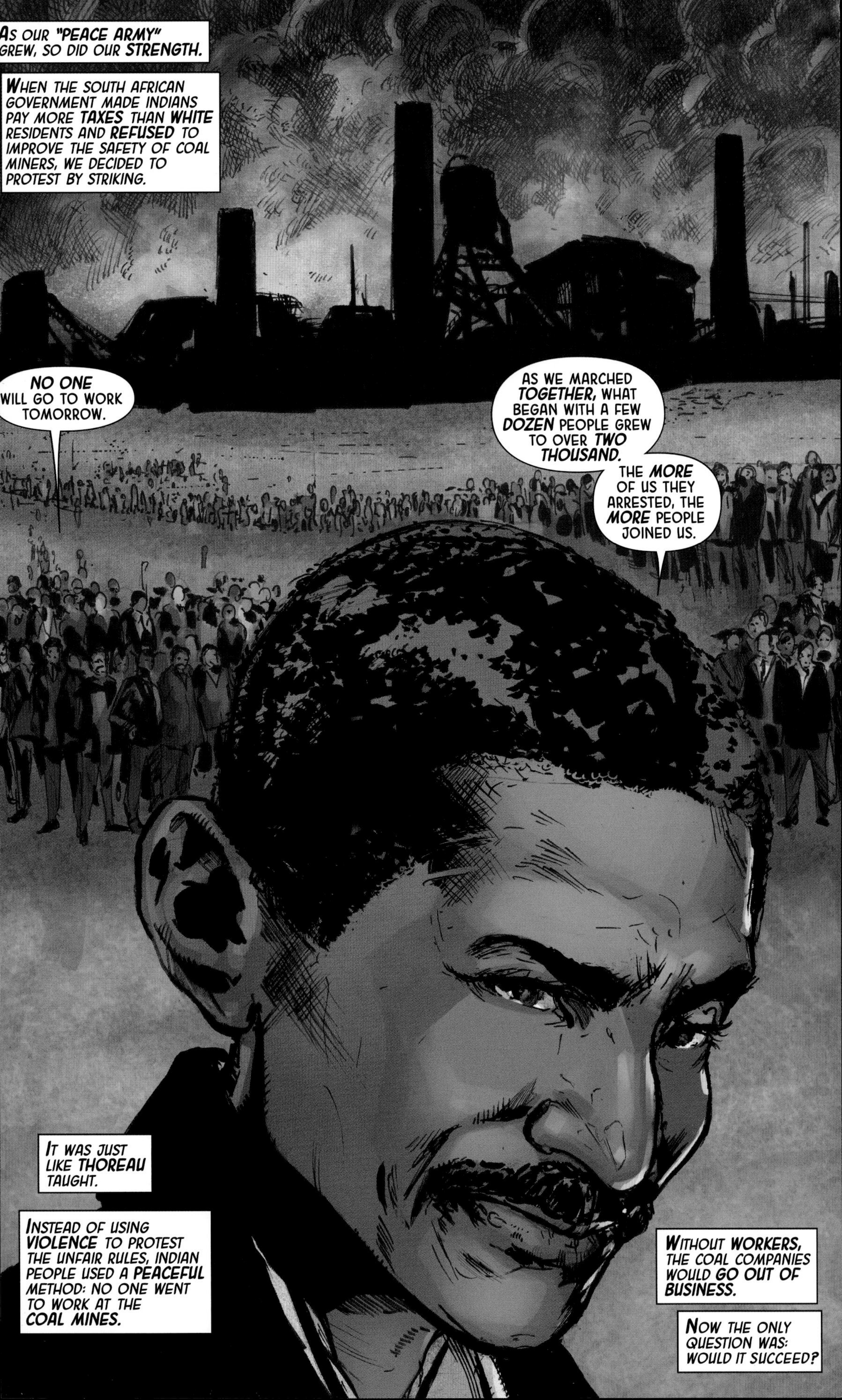
As our "PEACE ARMY" grew, so did our STRENGTH.
When the South African government made Indians pay more TAXES than WHITE residents and REFUSED to improve the safety of coal miners, we decided to protest by striking.
NO ONE WILL GO TO WORK TOMORROW.
AS WE MARCHED TOGETHER, WHAT BEGAN WITH A FEW DOZEN PEOPLE GREW TO OVER TWO THOUSAND.
THE MORE OF US THEY ARRESTED, THE MORE PEOPLE JOINED US.
It was just like THOREAU taught.
Instead of using VIOLENCE to protest the unfair rules, Indian people used a PEACEFUL method: no one went to work at the COAL MINES.
Without WORKERS, the coal companies would GO OUT OF BUSINESS.
Now the only question was: would it succeed?

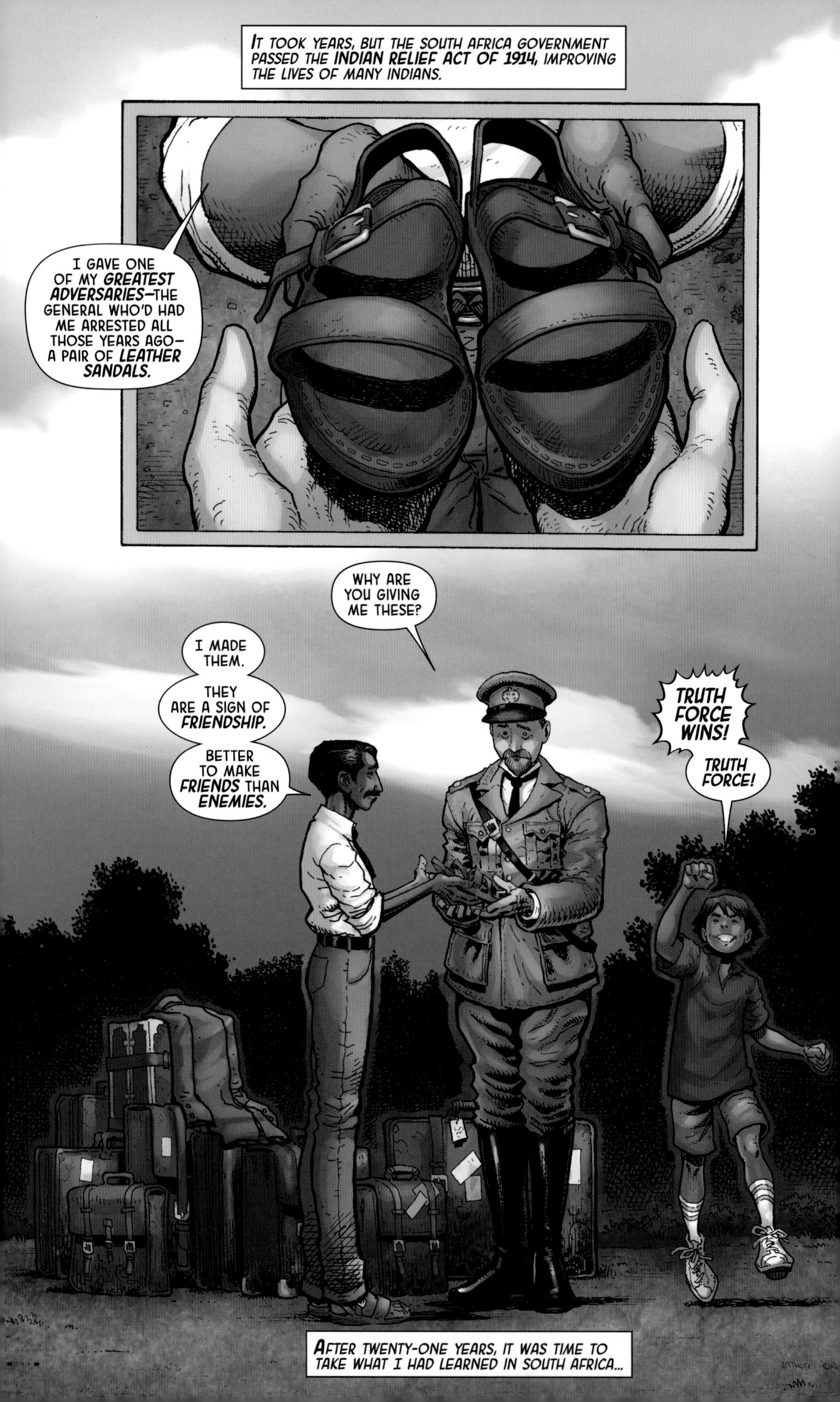
IT TOOK YEARS, BUT THE SOUTH AFRICA GOVERNMENT PASSED THE INDIAN RELIEF ACT OF 1914, IMPROVING THE LIVES OF MANY INDIANS.
I GAVE ONE OF MY GREATEST ADVERSARIES—THE GENERAL WHO'D HAD ME ARRESTED ALL THOSE YEARS AGO—A PAIR OF LEATHER SANDALS.
WHY ARE YOU GIVING ME THESE?
I MADE THEM.
THEY ARE A SIGN OF FRIENDSHIP.
BETTER TO MAKE FRIENDS THAN ENEMIES.
TRUTH FORCE WINS!
TRUTH FORCE!
AFTER TWENTY-ONE YEARS, IT WAS TIME TO TAKE WHAT I HAD LEARNED IN SOUTH AFRICA...

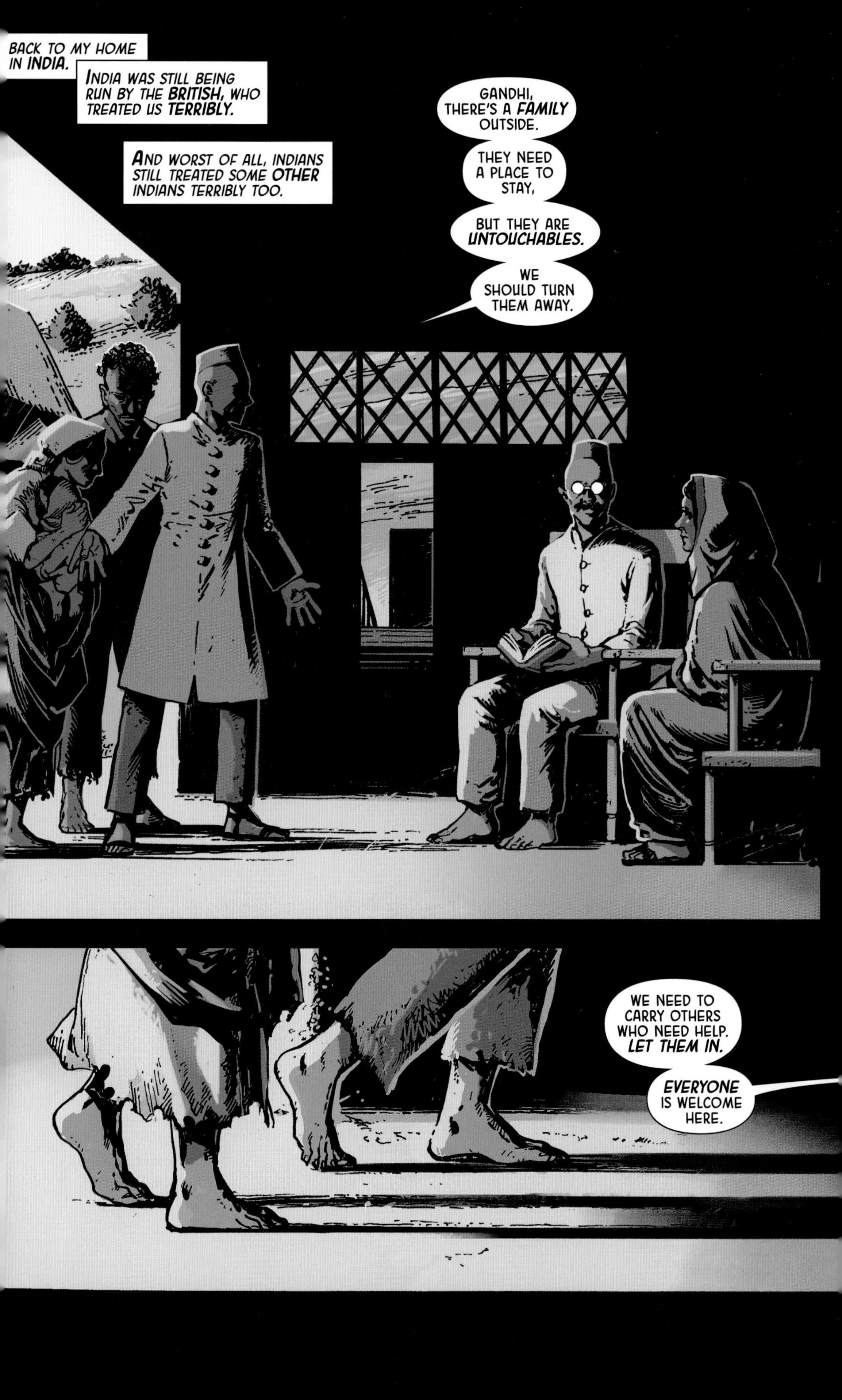

BACK TO MY HOME IN INDIA.
INDIA WAS STILL BEING RUN BY THE BRITISH, WHO TREATED US TERRIBLY.
AND WORST OF ALL, INDIANS STILL TREATED SOME OTHER INDIANS TERRIBLY TOO.
GANDHI, THERE'S A FAMILY OUTSIDE.
THEY NEED A PLACE TO STAY,
BUT THEY ARE UNTOUCHABLES.
WE SHOULD TURN THEM AWAY.
WE NEED TO CARRY OTHERS WHO NEED HELP. LET THEM IN.
EVERYONE IS WELCOME HERE.

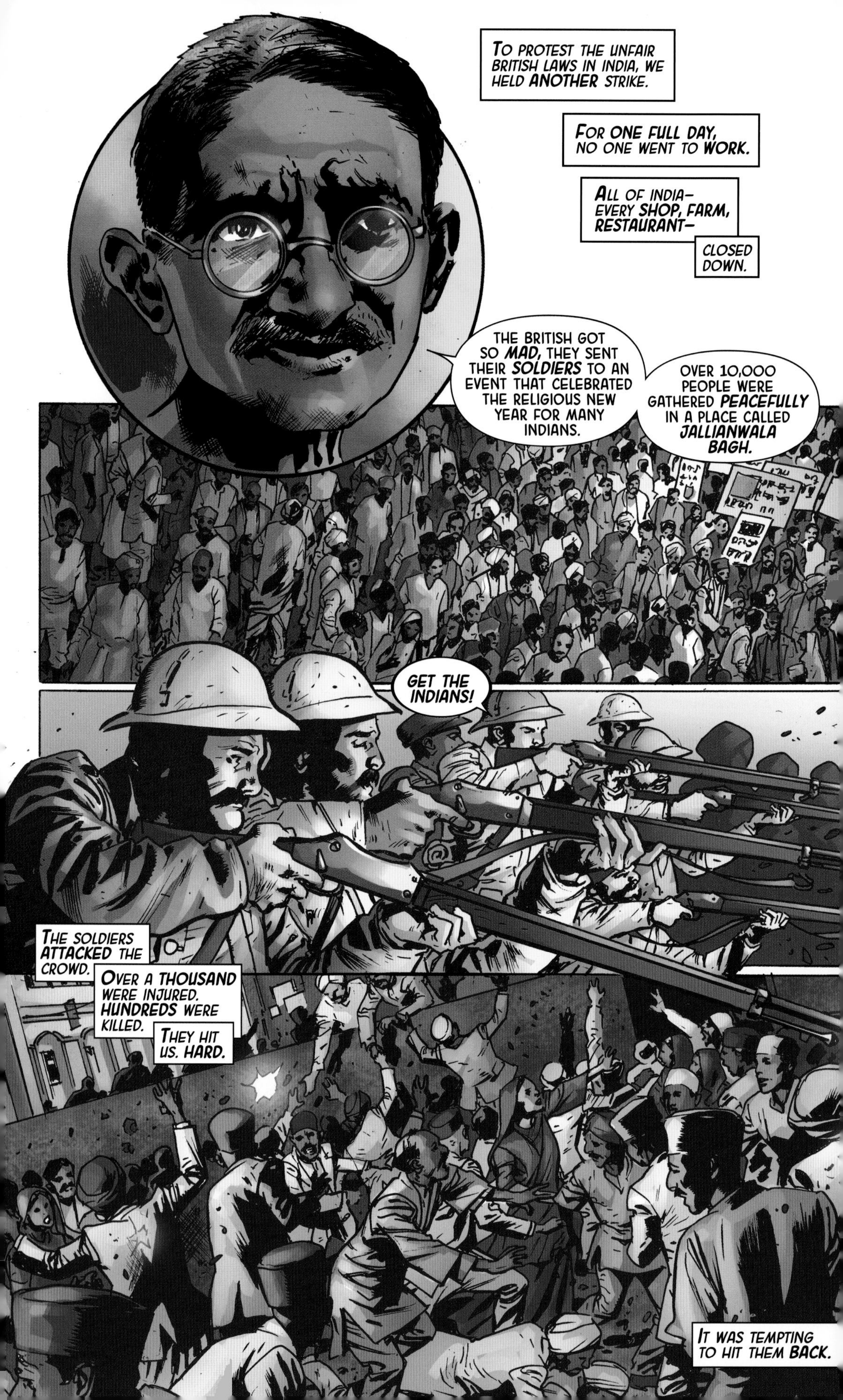

TO PROTEST THE UNFAIR BRITISH LAWS IN INDIA, WE HELD ANOTHER STRIKE.
FOR ONE FULL DAY, NO ONE WENT TO WORK.
ALL OF INDIA—EVERY SHOP, FARM, RESTAURANT—
CLOSED DOWN.
THE BRITISH GOT SO MAD, THEY SENT THEIR SOLDIERS TO AN EVENT THAT CELEBRATED THE RELIGIOUS NEW YEAR FOR MANY INDIANS.
OVER 10,000 PEOPLE WERE GATHERED PEACEFULLY IN A PLACE CALLED JALLIANWALA BAGH.
GET THE INDIANS!
THE SOLDIERS ATTACKED THE CROWD.
OVER A THOUSAND WERE INJURED. HUNDREDS WERE KILLED.
THEY HIT US. HARD.
IT WAS TEMPTING TO HIT THEM BACK.

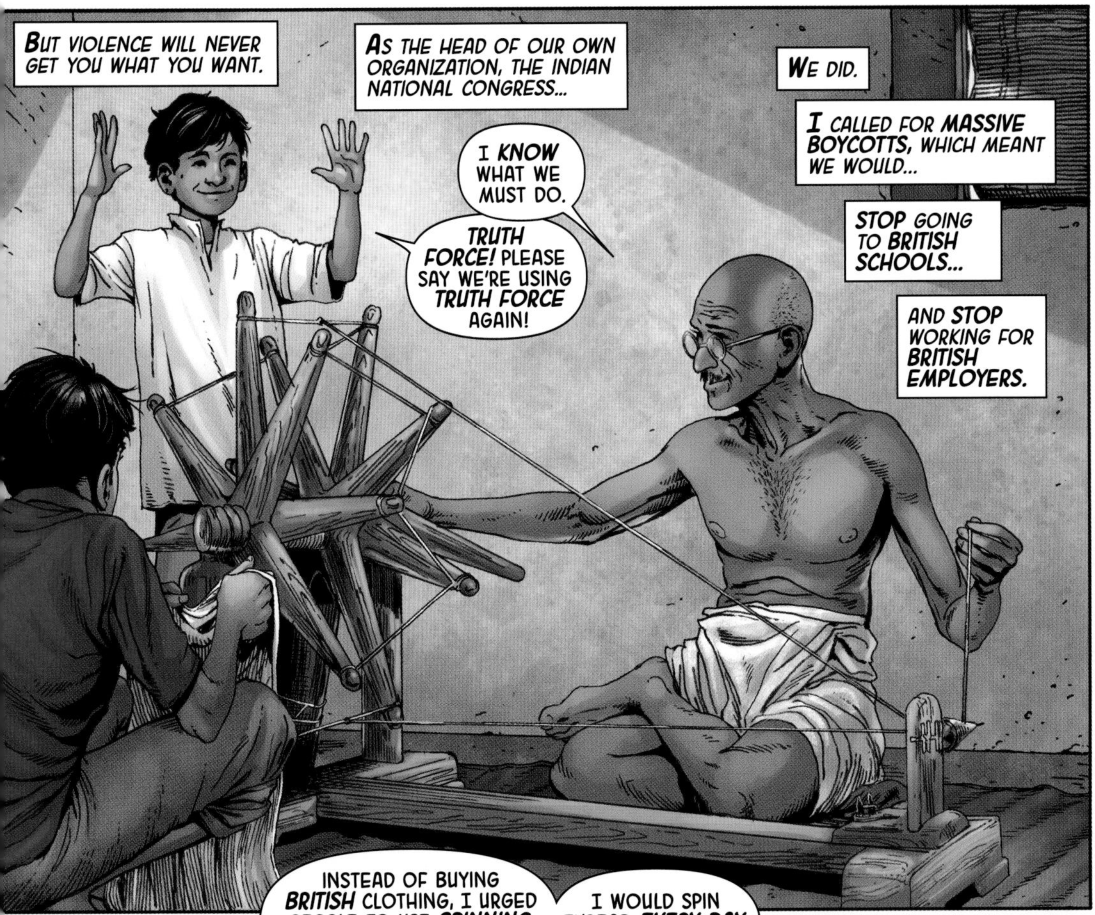
BUT VIOLENCE WILL NEVER GET YOU WHAT YOU WANT.
AS THE HEAD OF OUR OWN ORGANIZATION, THE INDIAN NATIONAL CONGRESS...
I KNOW WHAT WE MUST DO.
TRUTH FORCE! PLEASE SAY WE'RE USING TRUTH FORCE AGAIN!
WE DID.
I CALLED FOR MASSIVE BOYCOTTS, WHICH MEANT WE WOULD...
STOP GOING TO BRITISH SCHOOLS...
AND STOP WORKING FOR BRITISH EMPLOYERS.

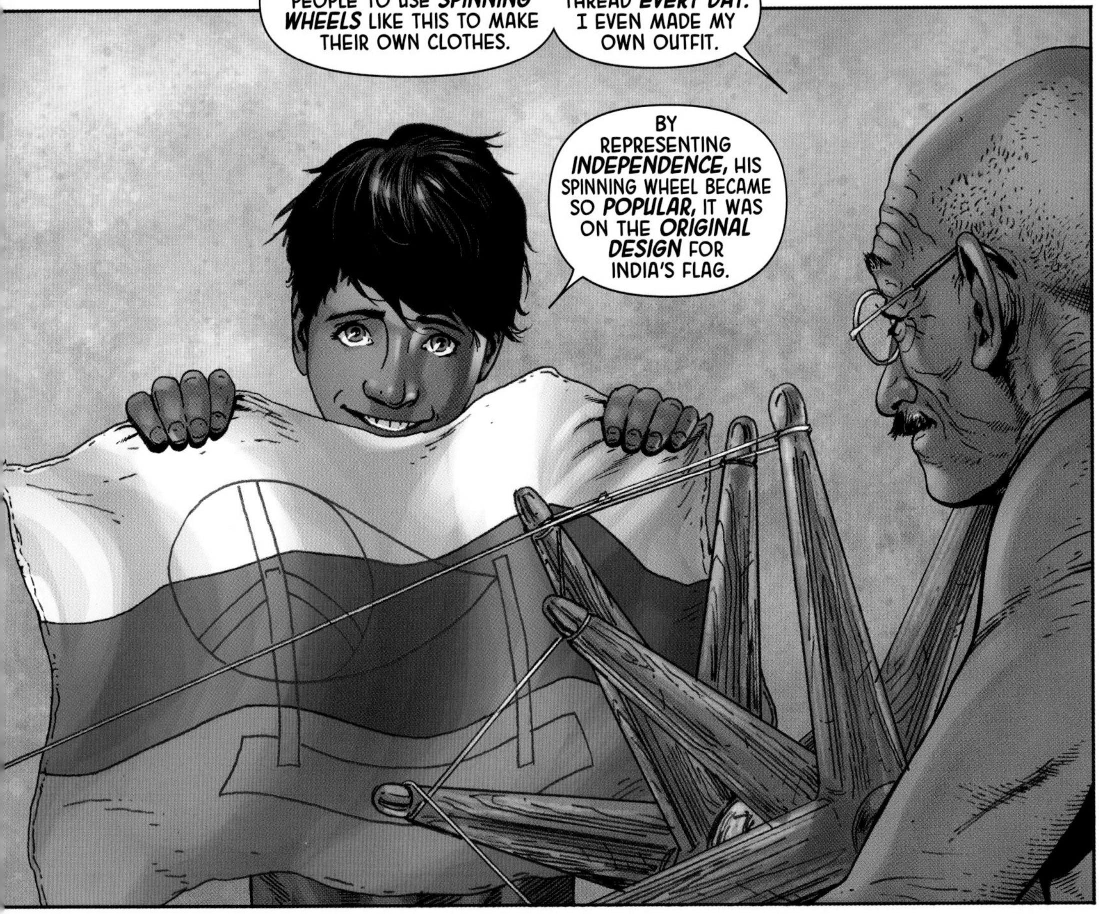
INSTEAD OF BUYING BRITISH CLOTHING, I URGED PEOPLE TO USE SPINNING WHEELS LIKE THIS TO MAKE THEIR OWN CLOTHES.
I WOULD SPIN THREAD EVERY DAY. I EVEN MADE MY OWN OUTFIT.
BY REPRESENTING INDEPENDENCE, HIS SPINNING WHEEL BECAME SO POPULAR, IT WAS ON THE ORIGINAL DESIGN FOR INDIA'S FLAG.

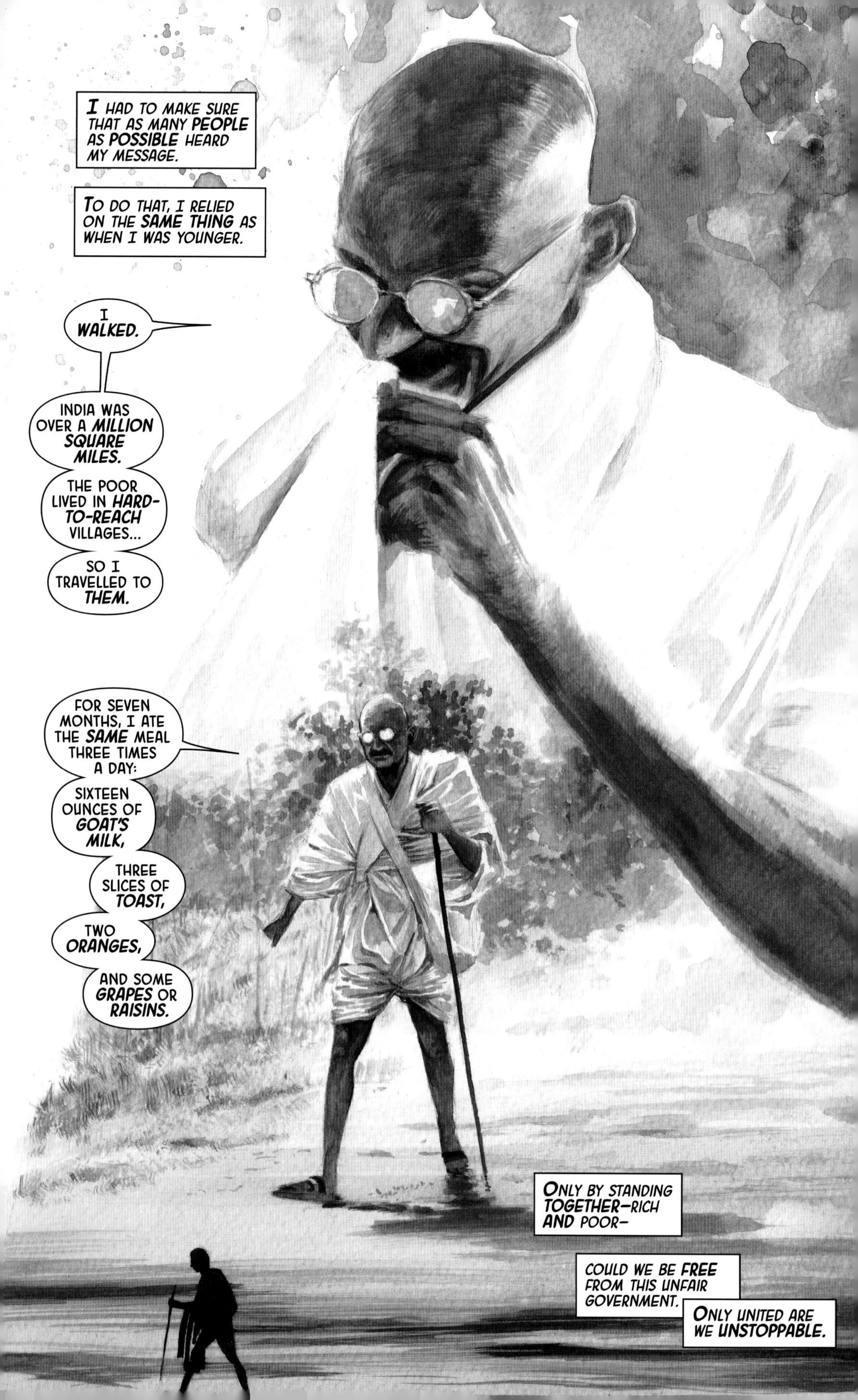

I HAD TO MAKE SURE THAT AS MANY PEOPLE AS POSSIBLE HEARD MY MESSAGE.
TO DO THAT, I RELIED ON THE SAME THING AS WHEN I WAS YOUNGER.
I WALKED.
INDIA WAS OVER A MILLION SQUARE MILES.
THE POOR LIVED IN HARD-TO-REACH VILLAGES...
SO I TRAVELLED TO THEM.
FOR SEVEN MONTHS, I ATE THE SAME MEAL THREE TIMES A DAY:
SIXTEEN OUNCES OF GOAT'S MILK,
THREE SLICES OF TOAST,
TWO ORANGES,
AND SOME GRAPES OR RAISINS.
ONLY BY STANDING TOGETHER—RICH AND POOR—
COULD WE BE FREE FROM THIS UNFAIR GOVERNMENT.
ONLY UNITED ARE WE UNSTOPPABLE.

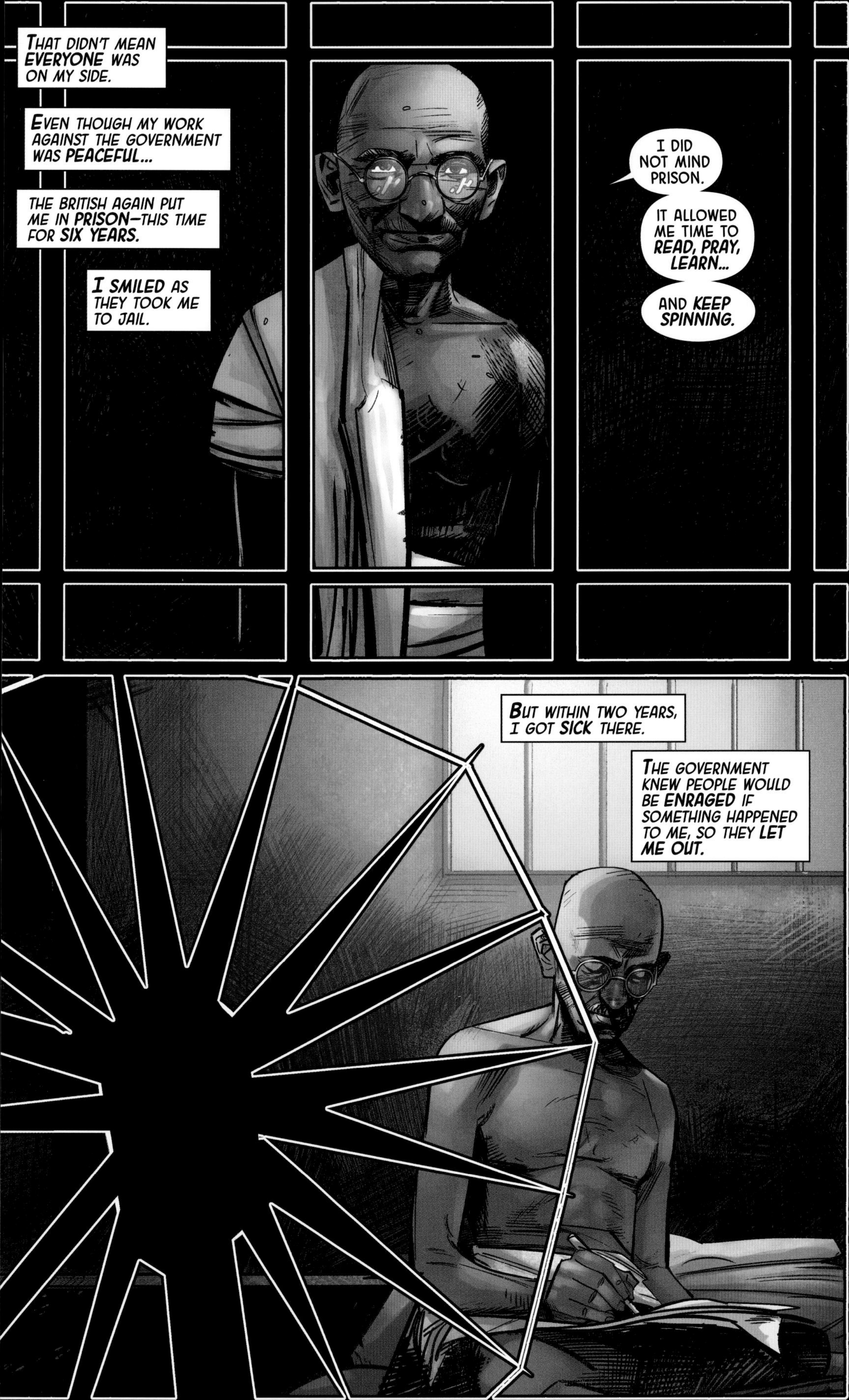
THAT DIDN'T MEAN EVERYONE WAS ON MY SIDE.
EVEN THOUGH MY WORK AGAINST THE GOVERNMENT WAS PEACEFUL...
THE BRITISH AGAIN PUT ME IN PRISON—THIS TIME FOR SIX YEARS.
I SMILED AS THEY TOOK ME TO JAIL.
I DID NOT MIND PRISON.
IT ALLOWED ME TIME TO READ, PRAY, LEARN...
AND KEEP SPINNING.
BUT WITHIN TWO YEARS, I GOT SICK THERE.
THE GOVERNMENT KNEW PEOPLE WOULD BE ENRAGED IF SOMETHING HAPPENED TO ME, SO THEY LET ME OUT.

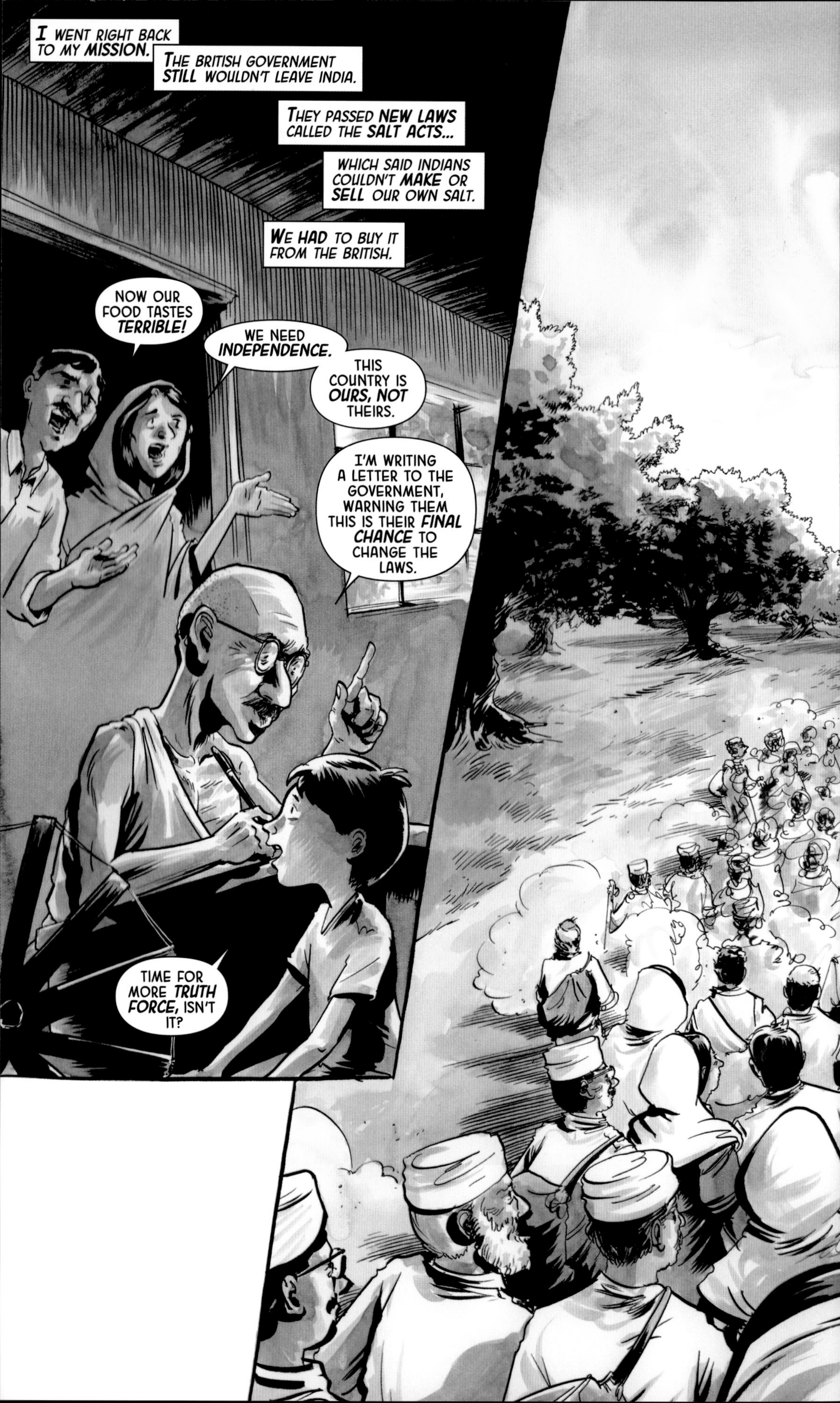
I WENT RIGHT BACK TO MY MISSION.
THE BRITISH GOVERNMENT STILL WOULDN'T LEAVE INDIA.
THEY PASSED NEW LAWS CALLED THE SALT ACTS...
WHICH SAID INDIANS COULDN'T MAKE OR SELL OUR OWN SALT.
WE HAD TO BUY IT FROM THE BRITISH.
NOW OUR FOOD TASTES TERRIBLE!
WE NEED INDEPENDENCE.
THIS COUNTRY IS OURS, NOT THEIRS.
I'M WRITING A LETTER TO THE GOVERNMENT, WARNING THEM THIS IS THEIR FINAL CHANCE TO CHANGE THE LAWS.
TIME FOR MORE TRUTH FORCE, ISN'T IT?

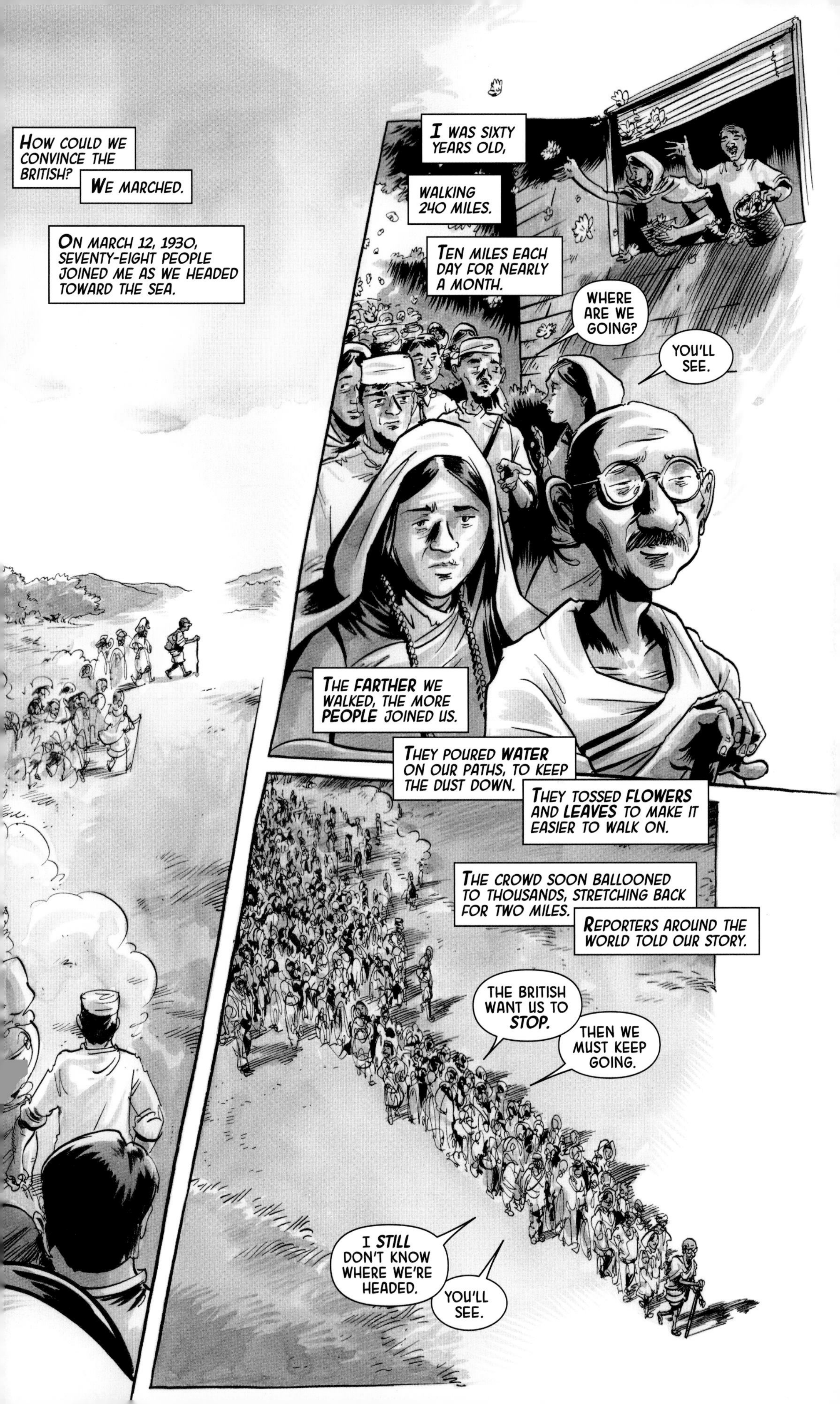

HOW COULD WE CONVINCE THE BRITISH?
WE MARCHED.
ON MARCH 12, 1930, SEVENTY-EIGHT PEOPLE JOINED ME AS WE HEADED TOWARD THE SEA.
I WAS SIXTY YEARS OLD,
WALKING 240 MILES.
TEN MILES EACH DAY FOR NEARLY A MONTH.
WHERE ARE WE GOING?
YOU'LL SEE.
THE FARTHER WE WALKED, THE MORE PEOPLE JOINED US.
THEY POURED WATER ON OUR PATHS, TO KEEP THE DUST DOWN.
THEY TOSSED FLOWERS AND LEAVES TO MAKE IT EASIER TO WALK ON.
THE CROWD SOON BALLOONED TO THOUSANDS, STRETCHING BACK FOR TWO MILES.
REPORTERS AROUND THE WORLD TOLD OUR STORY.
THE BRITISH WANT US TO STOP.
THEN WE MUST KEEP GOING.
I STILL DON'T KNOW WHERE WE'RE HEADED.
YOU'LL SEE.

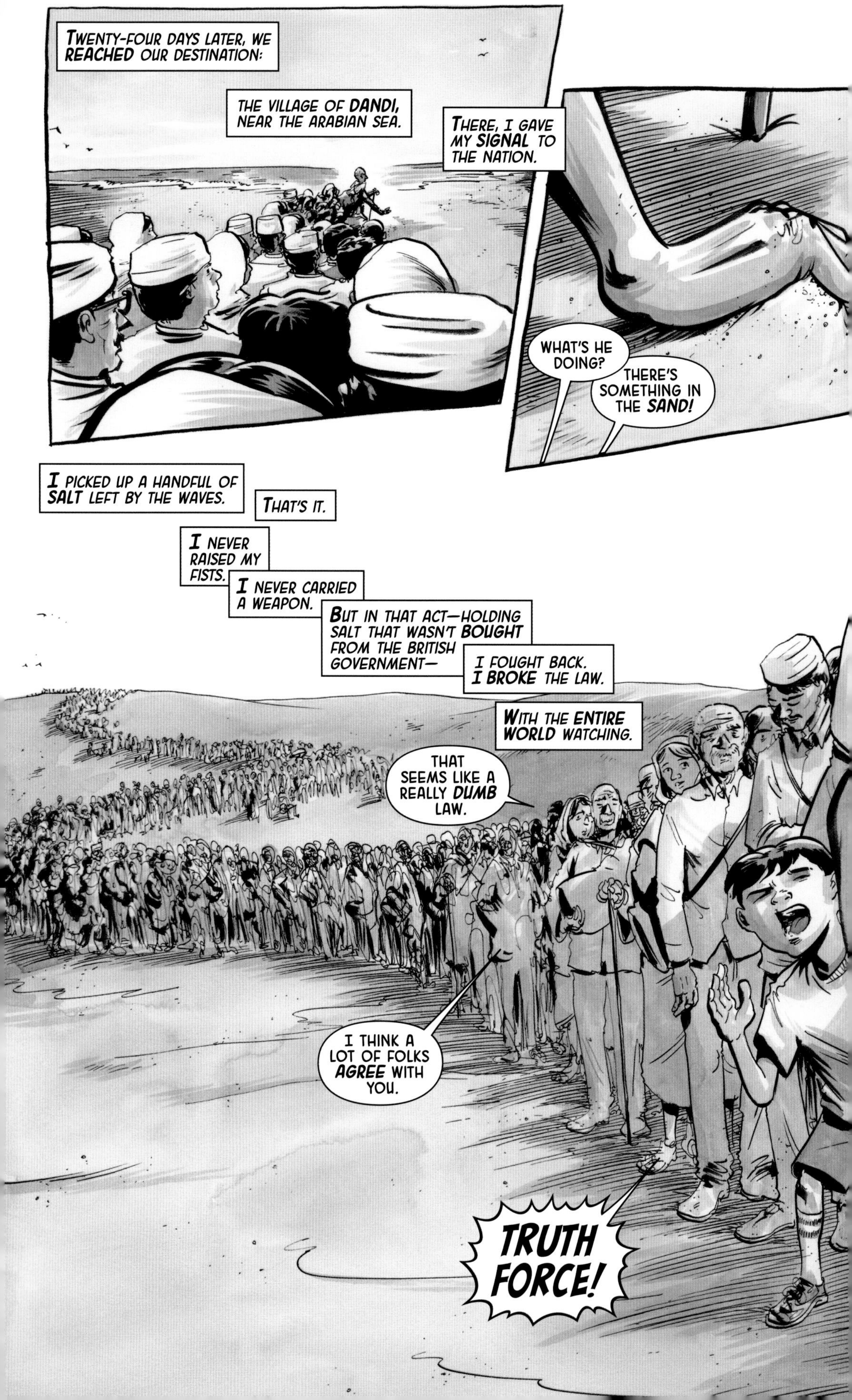
TWENTY-FOUR DAYS LATER, WE REACHED OUR DESTINATION:
THE VILLAGE OF DANDI, NEAR THE ARABIAN SEA.
THERE, I GAVE MY SIGNAL TO THE NATION.
WHAT'S HE DOING?
THERE'S SOMETHING IN THE SAND!
I PICKED UP A HANDFUL OF SALT LEFT BY THE WAVES.
THAT'S IT.
I NEVER RAISED MY FISTS.
I NEVER CARRIED A WEAPON.
BUT IN THAT ACT—HOLDING SALT THAT WASN'T BOUGHT FROM THE BRITISH GOVERNMENT—
I FOUGHT BACK. I BROKE THE LAW.
WITH THE ENTIRE WORLD WATCHING.
THAT SEEMS LIKE A REALLY DUMB LAW.
I THINK A LOT OF FOLKS AGREE WITH YOU.
TRUTH FORCE!

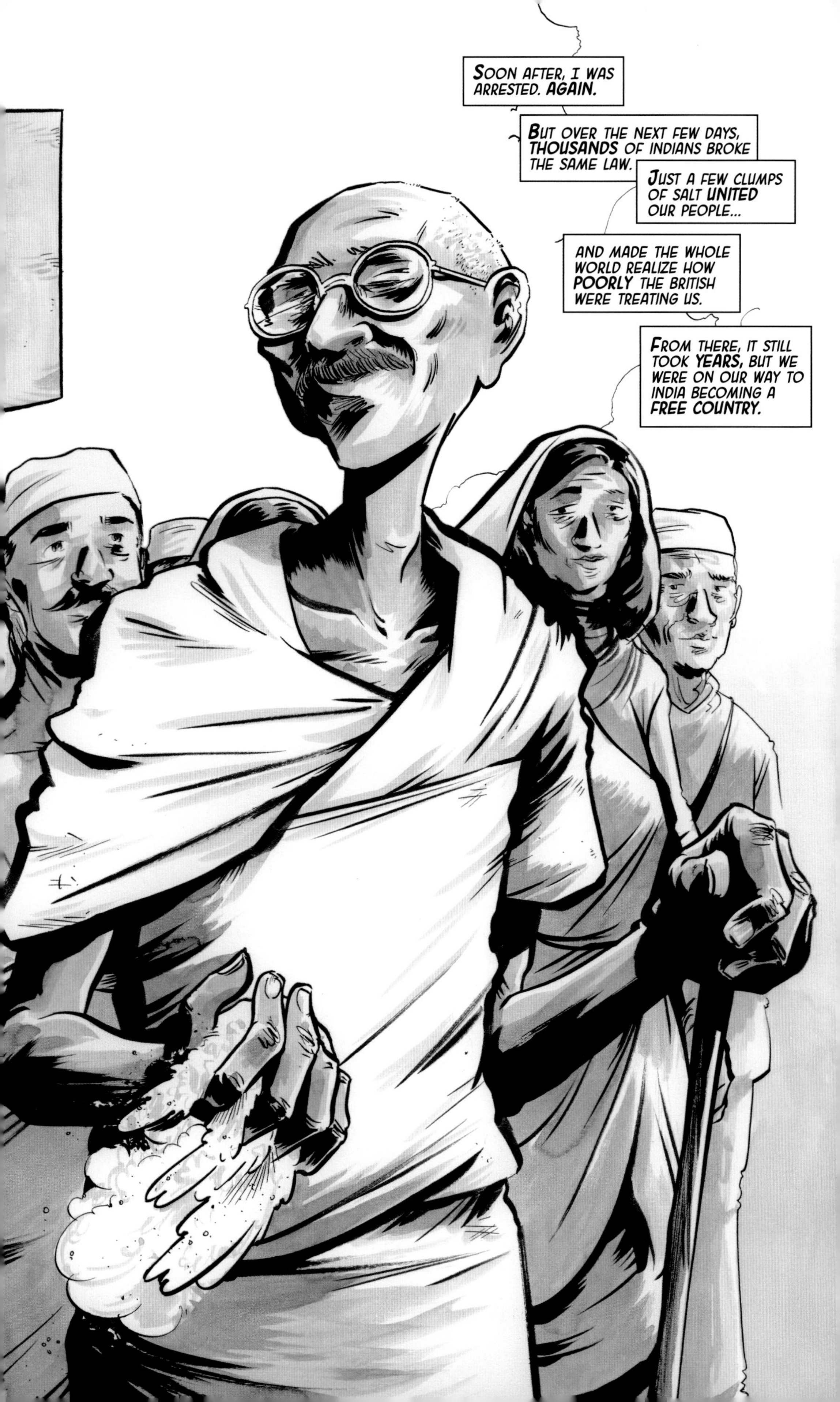
SOON AFTER, I WAS ARRESTED. AGAIN.
BUT OVER THE NEXT FEW DAYS, THOUSANDS OF INDIANS BROKE THE SAME LAW.
JUST A FEW CLUMPS OF SALT UNITED OUR PEOPLE...
AND MADE THE WHOLE WORLD REALIZE HOW POORLY THE BRITISH WERE TREATING US.
FROM THERE, IT STILL TOOK YEARS, BUT WE WERE ON OUR WAY TO INDIA BECOMING A FREE COUNTRY.

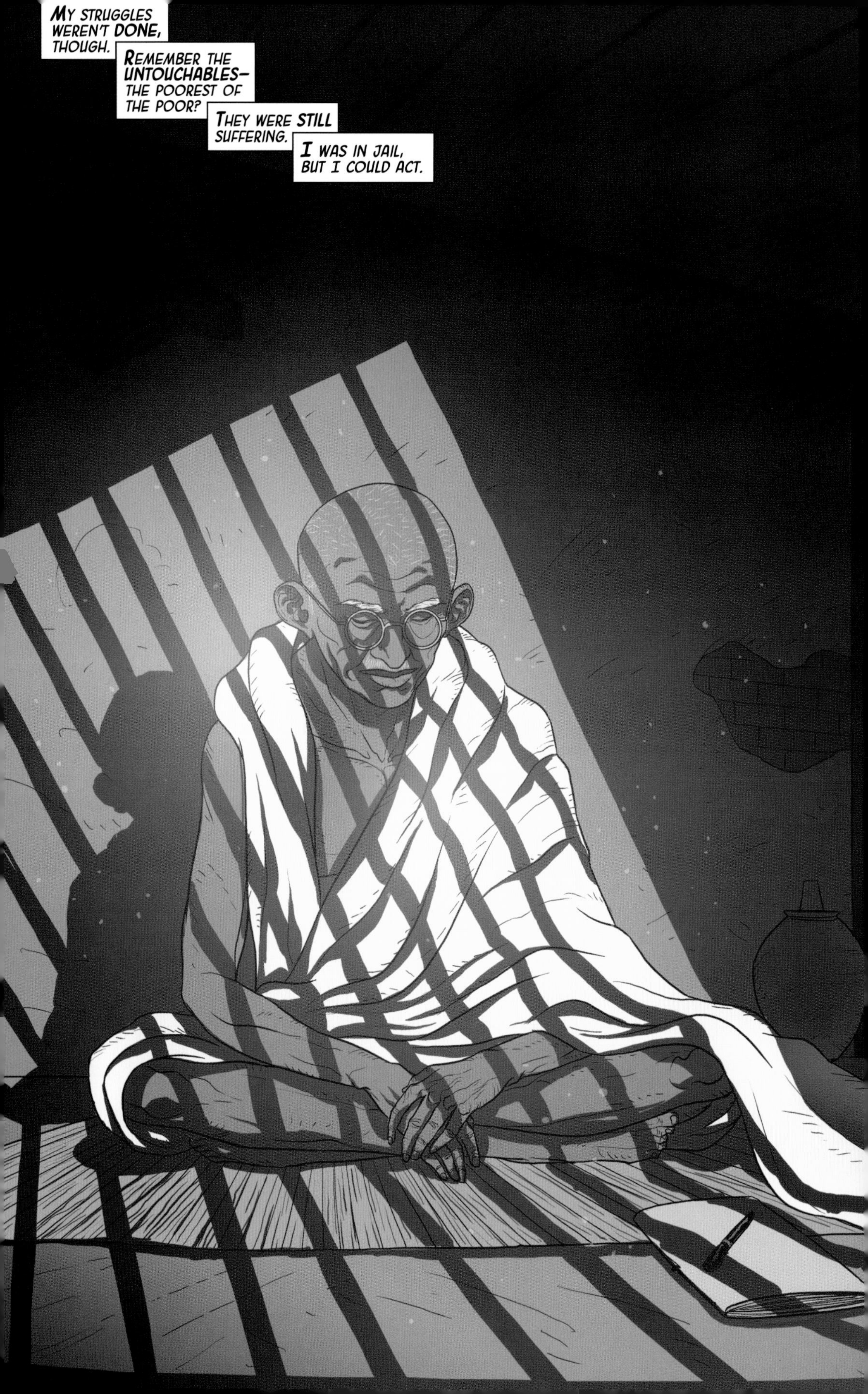
My struggles weren't DONE, though.
Remember the UNTOUCHABLES— the poorest of the poor?
They were STILL suffering.
I was in jail, but I could act.

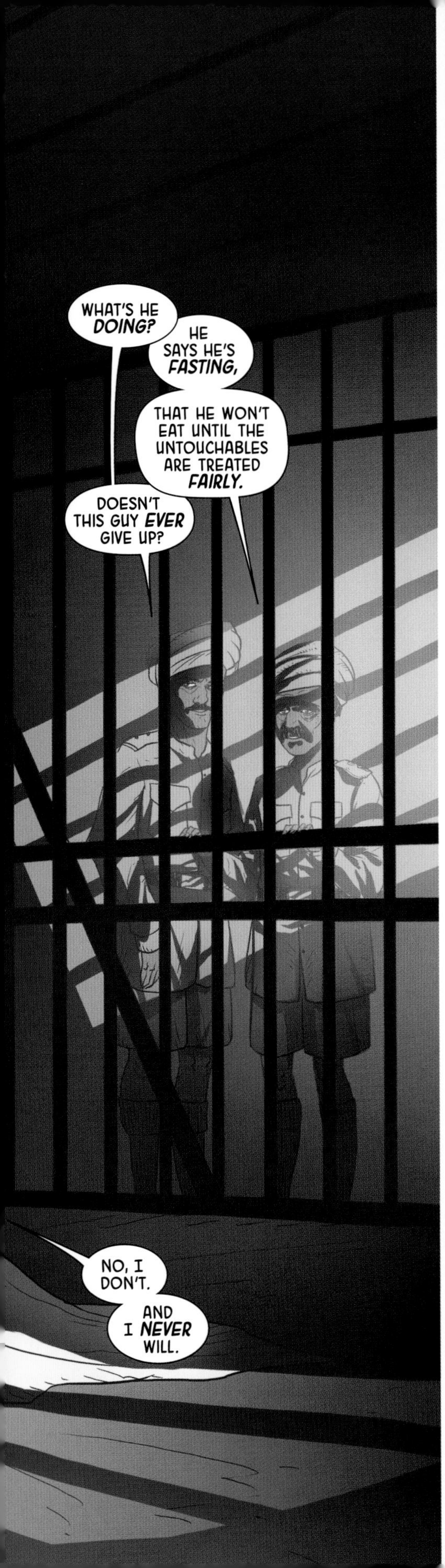
WHAT'S HE *DOING?*
HE SAYS HE'S *FASTING,*
THAT HE WON'T EAT UNTIL THE UNTOUCHABLES ARE TREATED *FAIRLY.*
DOESN'T THIS GUY *EVER* GIVE UP?
NO, I DON'T.
AND I *NEVER* WILL.

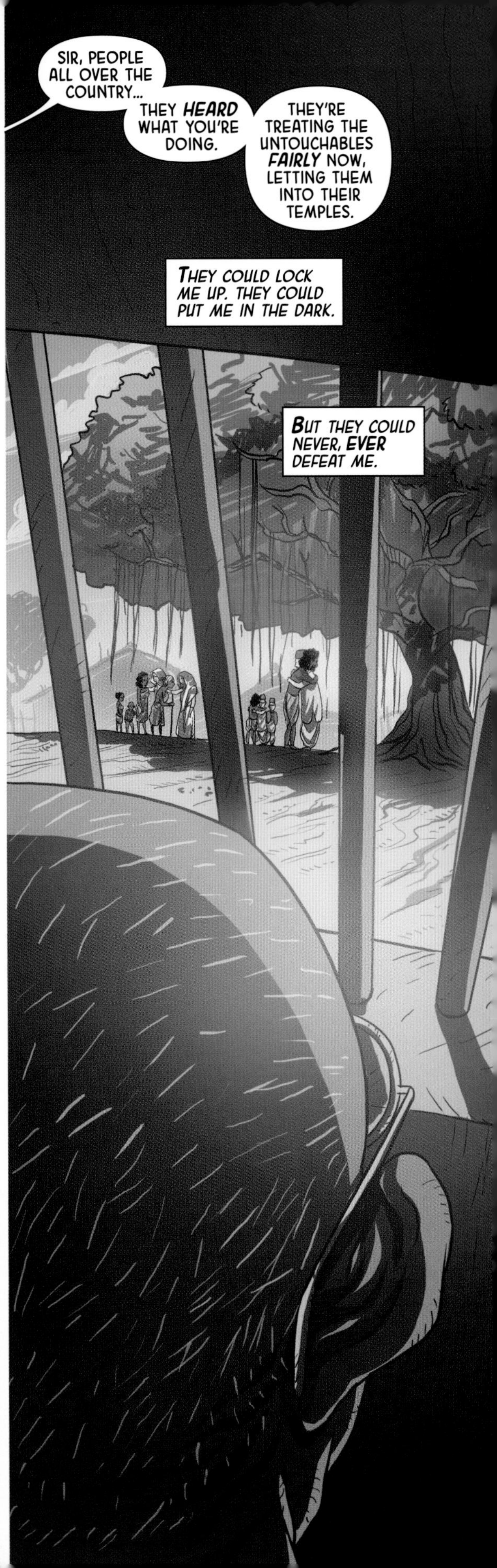
SIR, PEOPLE ALL OVER THE COUNTRY...
THEY *HEARD* WHAT YOU'RE DOING.
THEY'RE TREATING THE UNTOUCHABLES *FAIRLY* NOW, LETTING THEM INTO THEIR TEMPLES.
THEY COULD LOCK ME UP. THEY COULD PUT ME IN THE DARK.
BUT THEY COULD NEVER, EVER DEFEAT ME.

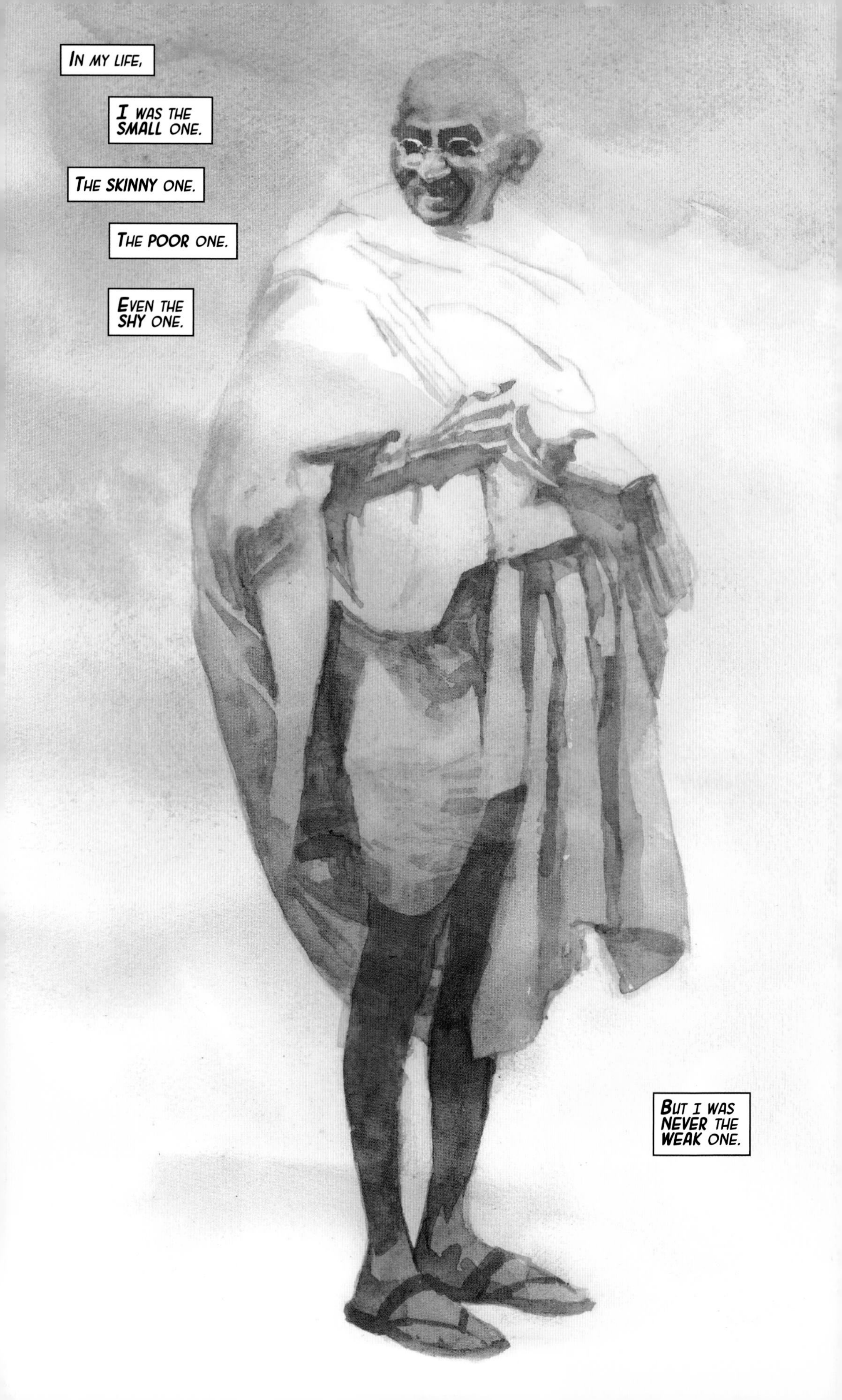
IN MY LIFE,
I WAS THE SMALL ONE.
THE SKINNY ONE.
THE POOR ONE.
EVEN THE SHY ONE.
BUT I WAS NEVER THE WEAK ONE.

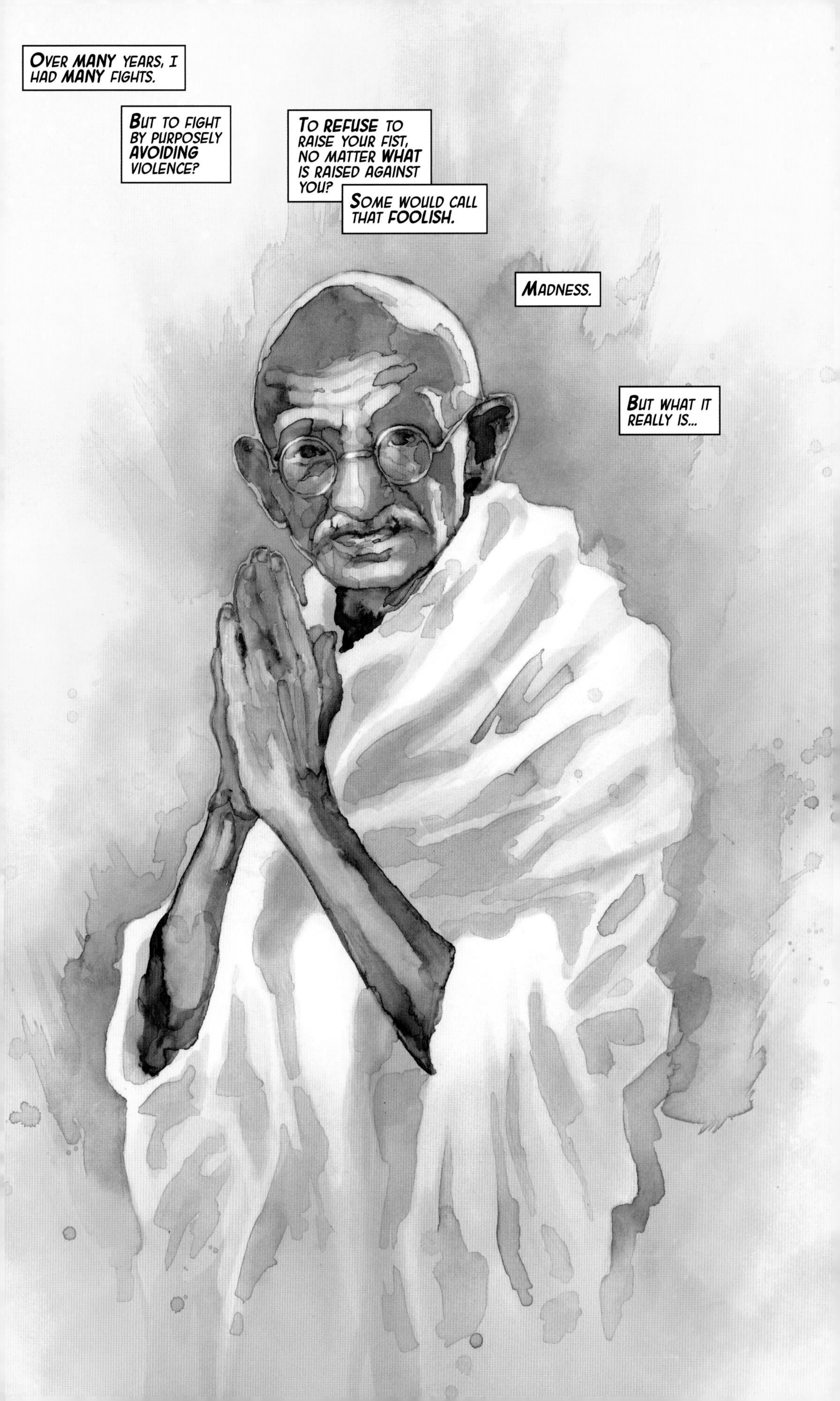

OVER MANY YEARS, I HAD MANY FIGHTS.
BUT TO FIGHT BY PURPOSELY AVOIDING VIOLENCE?
TO REFUSE TO RAISE YOUR FIST, NO MATTER WHAT IS RAISED AGAINST YOU?
SOME WOULD CALL THAT FOOLISH.
MADNESS.
BUT WHAT IT REALLY IS...

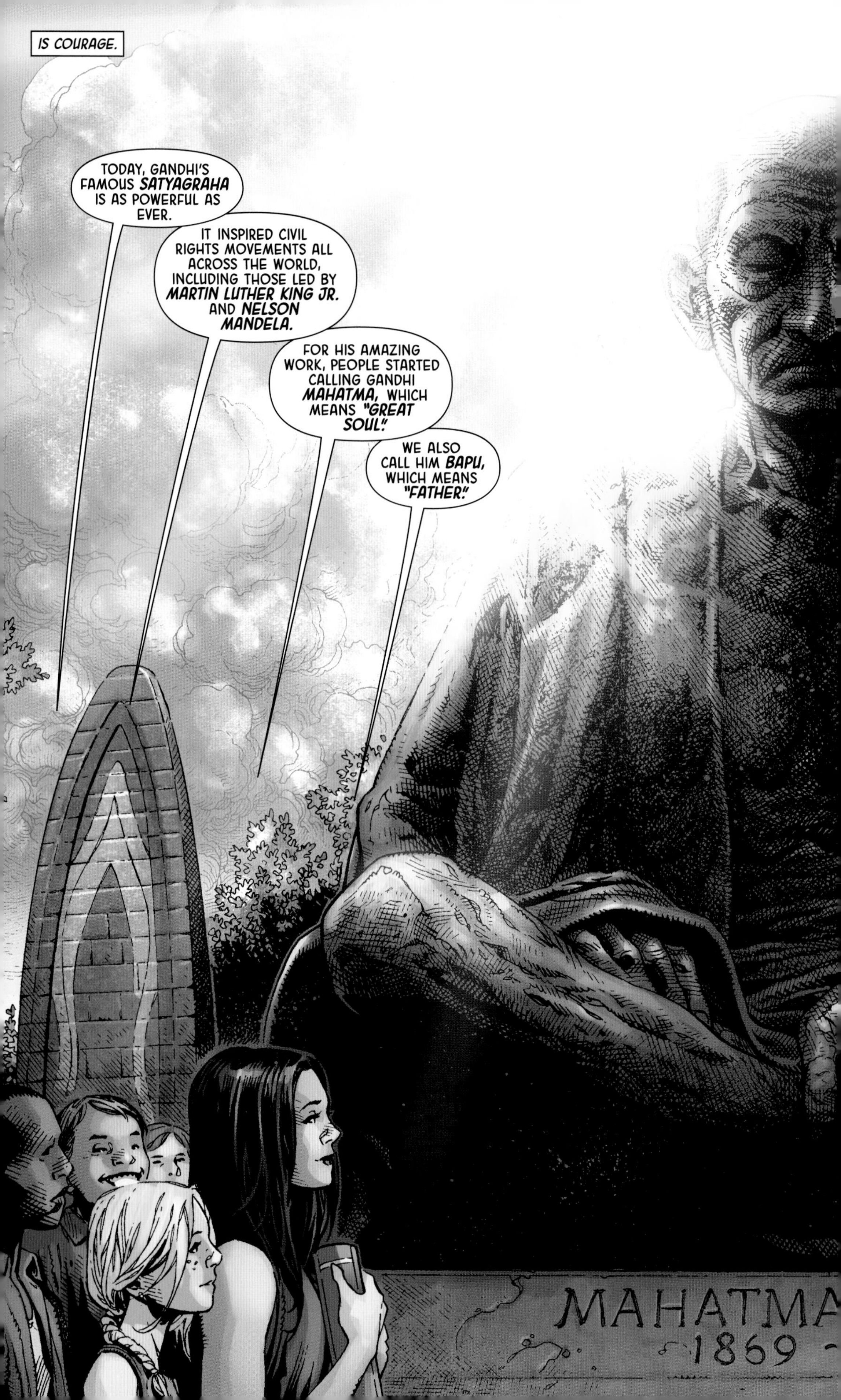

IS COURAGE.
TODAY, GANDHI'S FAMOUS SATYAGRAHA IS AS POWERFUL AS EVER.
IT INSPIRED CIVIL RIGHTS MOVEMENTS ALL ACROSS THE WORLD, INCLUDING THOSE LED BY MARTIN LUTHER KING JR. AND NELSON MANDELA.
FOR HIS AMAZING WORK, PEOPLE STARTED CALLING GANDHI MAHATMA, WHICH MEANS "GREAT SOUL."
WE ALSO CALL HIM BAPU, WHICH MEANS "FATHER."
MAHATMA
1869

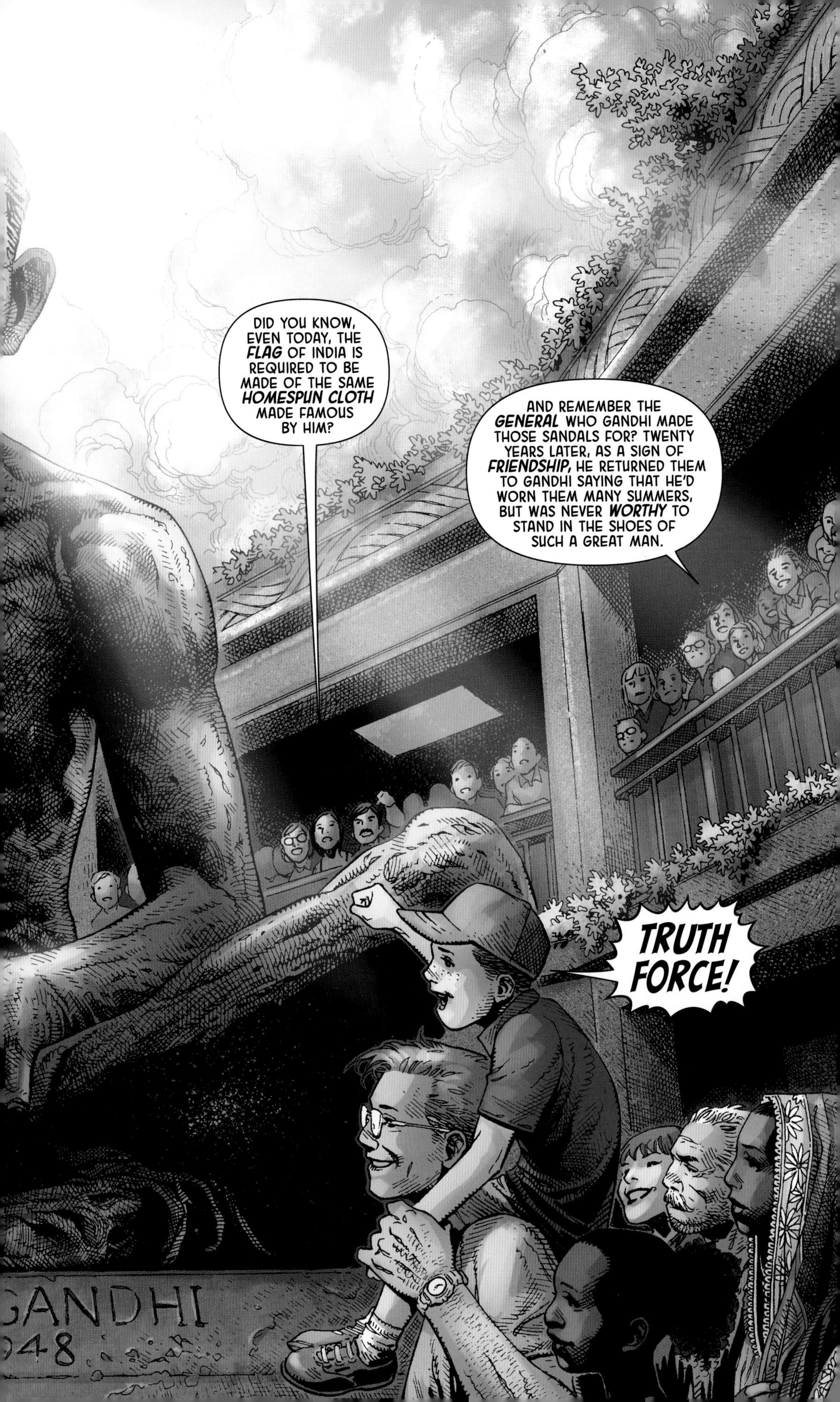
DID YOU KNOW, EVEN TODAY, THE FLAG OF INDIA IS REQUIRED TO BE MADE OF THE SAME HOMESPUN CLOTH MADE FAMOUS BY HIM?
AND REMEMBER THE GENERAL WHO GANDHI MADE THOSE SANDALS FOR? TWENTY YEARS LATER, AS A SIGN OF FRIENDSHIP, HE RETURNED THEM TO GANDHI SAYING THAT HE'D WORN THEM MANY SUMMERS, BUT WAS NEVER WORTHY TO STAND IN THE SHOES OF SUCH A GREAT MAN.
TRUTH FORCE!
GANDHI
948

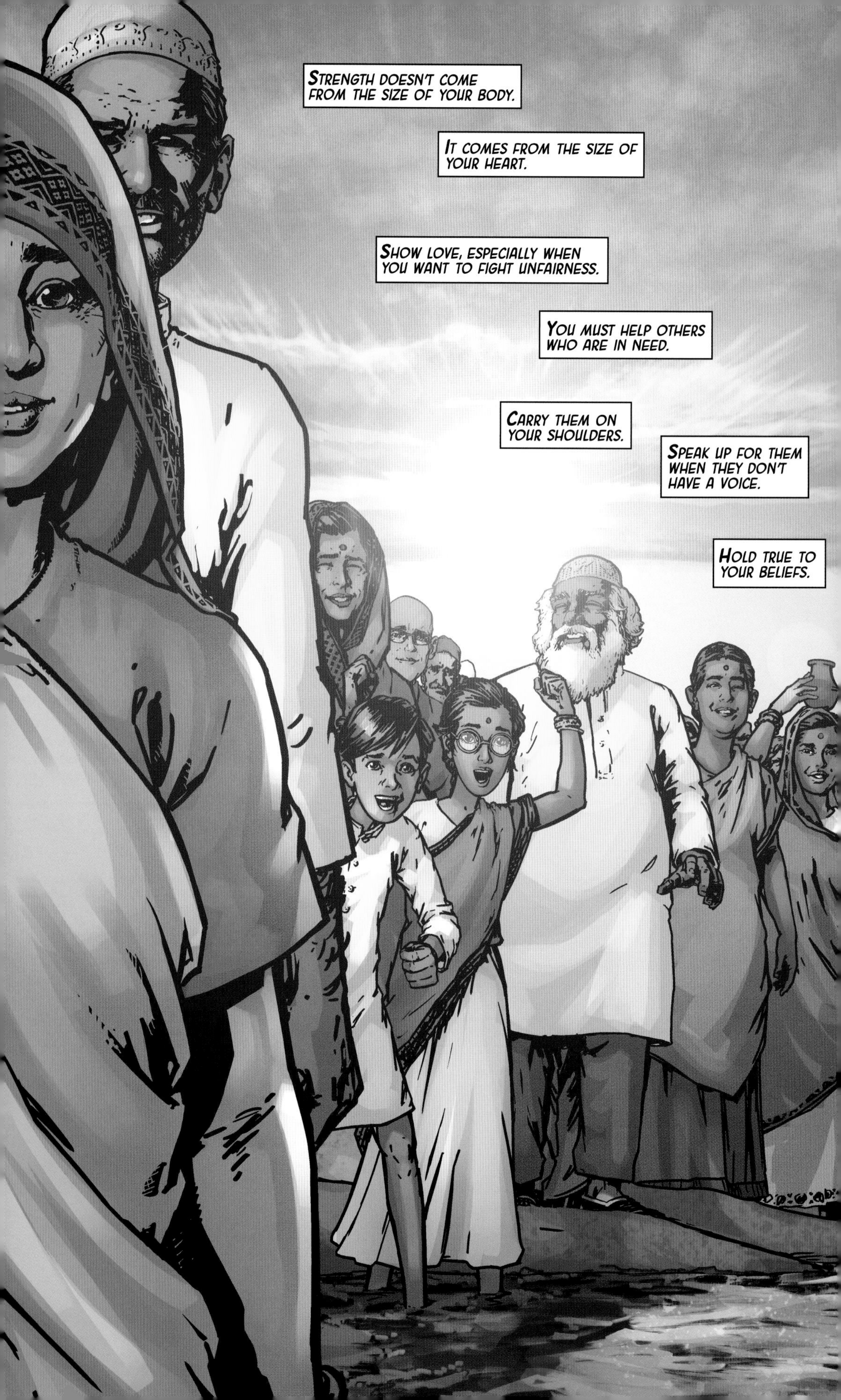
STRENGTH DOESN'T COME FROM THE SIZE OF YOUR BODY.
IT COMES FROM THE SIZE OF YOUR HEART.
SHOW LOVE, ESPECIALLY WHEN YOU WANT TO FIGHT UNFAIRNESS.
YOU MUST HELP OTHERS WHO ARE IN NEED.
CARRY THEM ON YOUR SHOULDERS.
SPEAK UP FOR THEM WHEN THEY DON'T HAVE A VOICE.
HOLD TRUE TO YOUR BELIEFS.

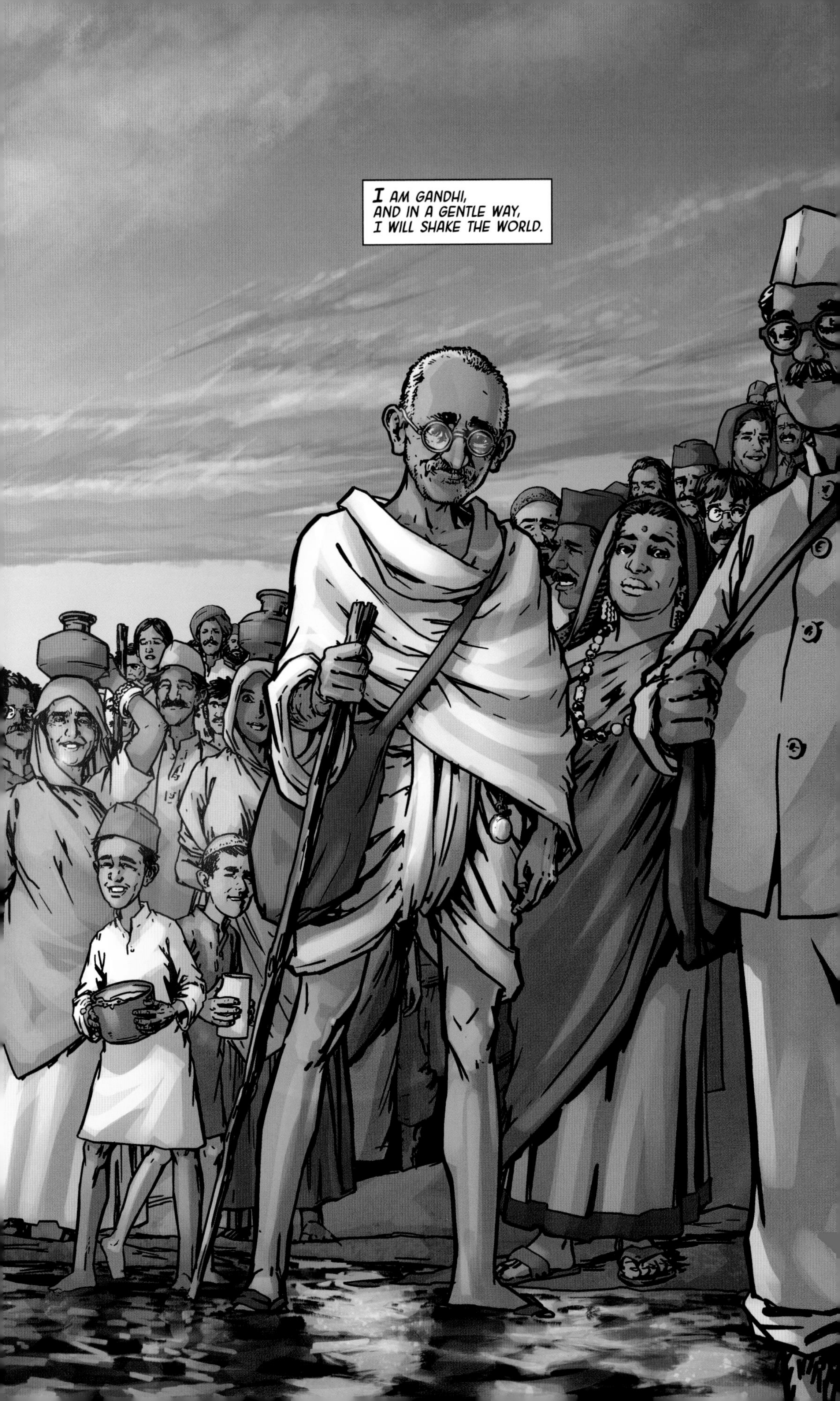
I AM GANDHI,
AND IN A GENTLE WAY,
I WILL SHAKE THE WORLD.

"STRENGTH DOES NOT COME FROM PHYSICAL CAPACITY. IT COMES FROM AN INDOMITABLE WILL."

"FREEDOM IS NOT WORTH HAVING IF IT DOES NOT CONNOTE THE FREEDOM TO ERR."

◆

"IN A GENTLE WAY, YOU CAN SHAKE THE WORLD."

"THE PATH OF TRUE NON-VIOLENCE REQUIRES MUCH MORE COURAGE THAN VIOLENCE."

◆

"I DO NOT ACCEPT THE CLAIM OF SAINTLINESS... I AM PRONE TO AS MANY WEAKNESSES AS YOU ARE. BUT I HAVE SEEN THE WORLD. I HAVE LIVED IN THE WORLD WITH MY EYES OPEN."

◆

"THE STRENGTH OF A WARRIOR IS NOT MEASURED BY REFERENCE TO HIS WEAPONS BUT BY HIS FIRMNESS OF MIND."

◆

"FOR MEN LIKE ME, YOU HAVE TO MEASURE THEM NOT BY THE RARE MOMENTS OF GREATNESS IN THEIR LIVES, BUT BY THE AMOUNT OF DUST THEY COLLECT ON THEIR FEET IN THE COURSE OF LIFE'S JOURNEY."

Timeline

OCTOBER 2, 1869

Born in
Porbandar, India

FEBRUARY 22, 1944

His wife, Kasturba (who
had been arrested with
him), dies in prison

MAY 6, 1944

Released from prison for
health reasons

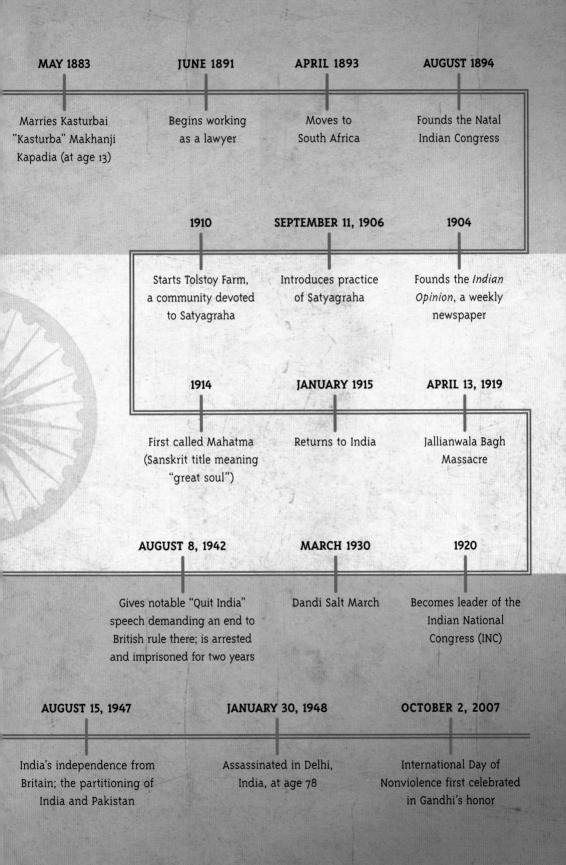

MAY 1883
Marries Kasturbai "Kasturba" Makhanji Kapadia (at age 13)

JUNE 1891
Begins working as a lawyer

APRIL 1893
Moves to South Africa

AUGUST 1894
Founds the Natal Indian Congress

1910
Starts Tolstoy Farm, a community devoted to Satyagraha

SEPTEMBER 11, 1906
Introduces practice of Satyagraha

1904
Founds the *Indian Opinion*, a weekly newspaper

1914
First called Mahatma (Sanskrit title meaning "great soul")

JANUARY 1915
Returns to India

APRIL 13, 1919
Jallianwala Bagh Massacre

AUGUST 8, 1942
Gives notable "Quit India" speech demanding an end to British rule there; is arrested and imprisoned for two years

MARCH 1930
Dandi Salt March

1920
Becomes leader of the Indian National Congress (INC)

AUGUST 15, 1947
India's independence from Britain; the partitioning of India and Pakistan

JANUARY 30, 1948
Assassinated in Delhi, India, at age 78

OCTOBER 2, 2007
International Day of Nonviolence first celebrated in Gandhi's honor

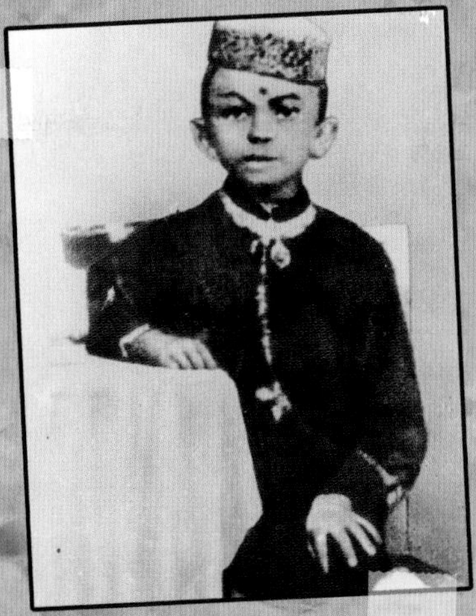

Gandhi at age seven

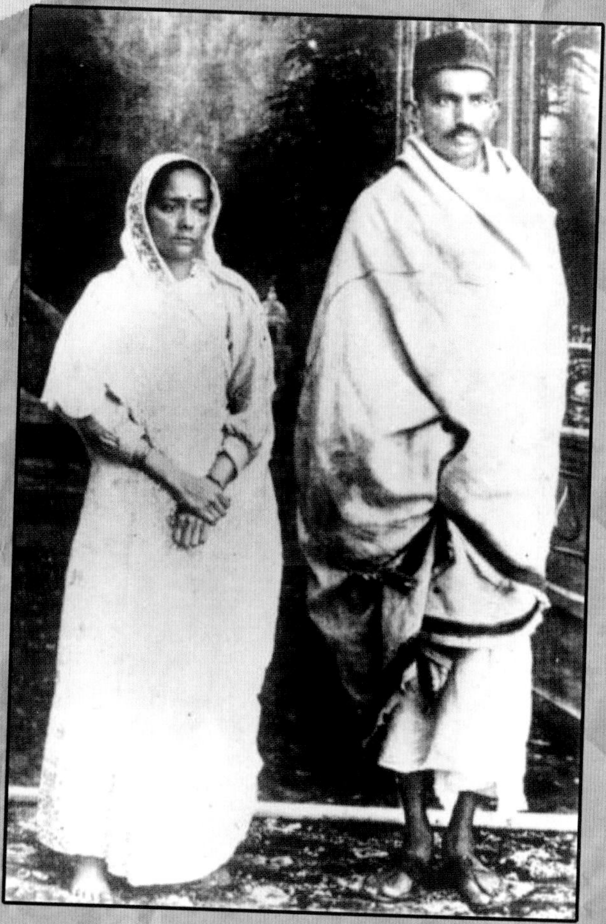

Gandhi with his wife, Kasturba (1922)

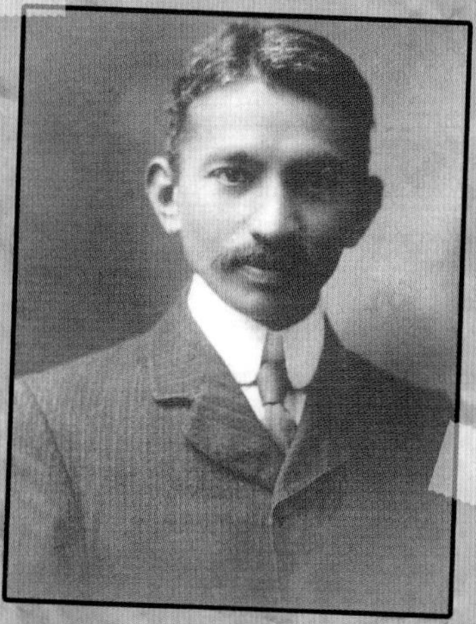

Gandhi at age forty

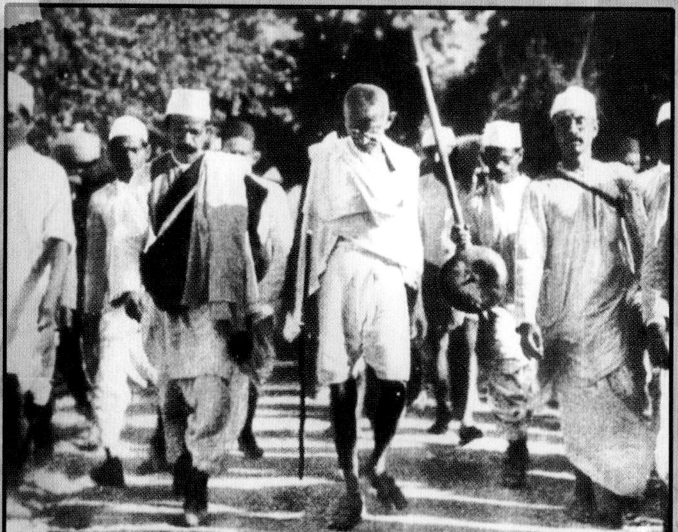

The Salt March

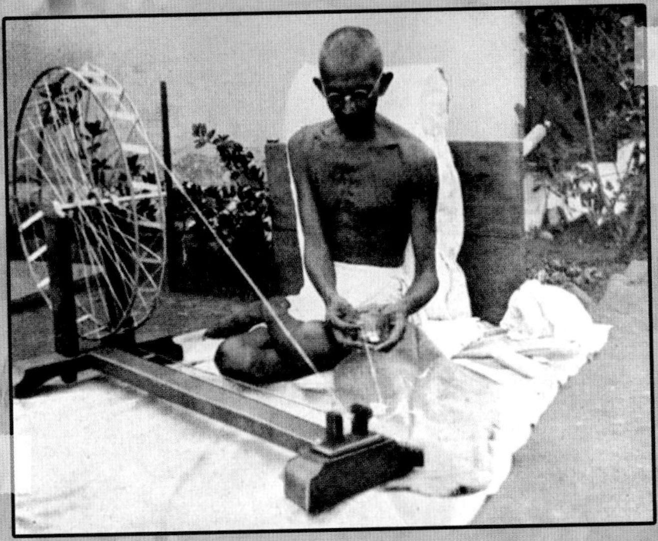

Gandhi at his spinning wheel (1940s)

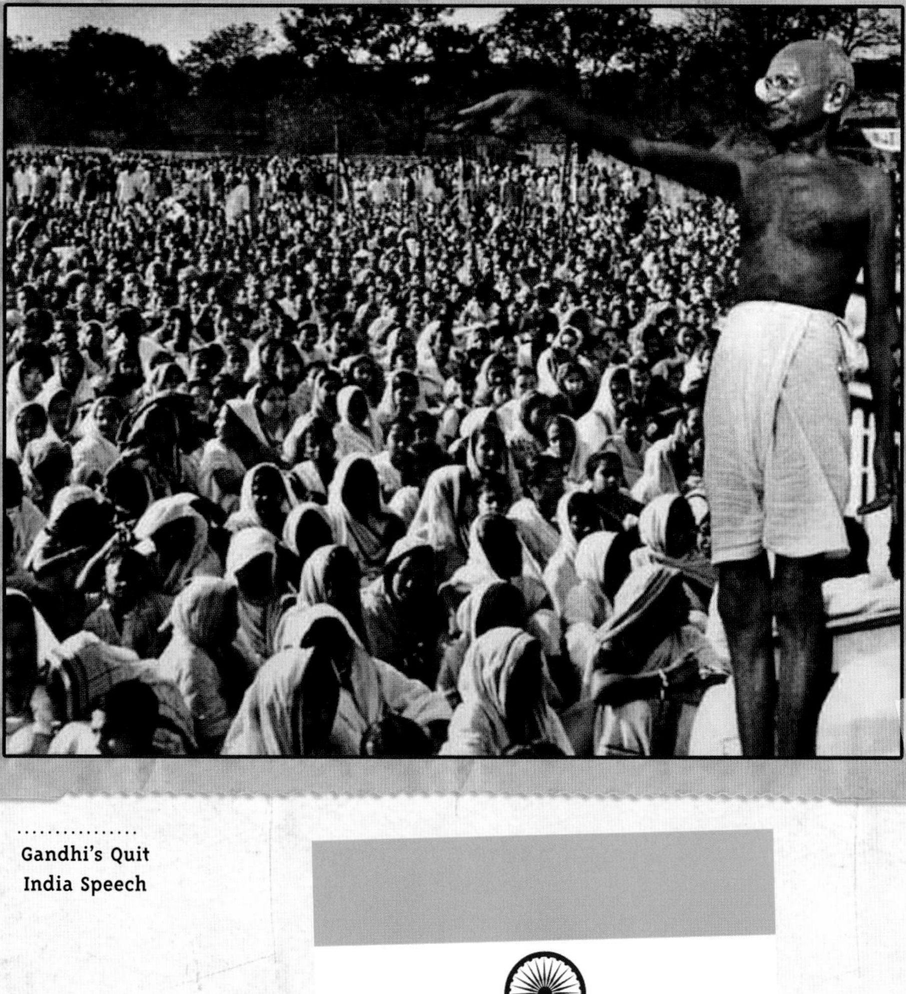

Gandhi's Quit India Speech

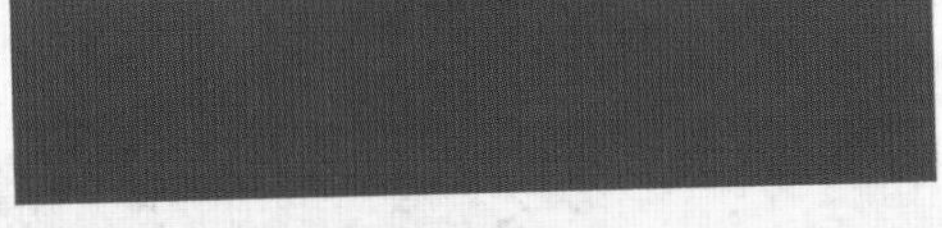

The current Indian flag

Sources

Gandhi, An Autobiography—The Story of My Experiments With Truth by Mahatma Gandhi (Beacon Press, 1993).

Non-Violent Resistance (Satyagraha) by M. K. Gandhi (Dover, 2001).

Gandhi: His Life and Message for the World by Louis Fischer (Signet, 2010).

Gandhi by Peter Rühe (Phaidon Press, 2001).

The Mahatma Gandhi Canadian Foundation for World Peace: www.gandhifoundation.ca

Further Reading

The Essential Gandhi: An Anthology of His Writings on His Life, Work, and Ideas by Mahatma Gandhi (Vintage, 2002).

Walden and "Civil Disobedience" by Henry David Thoreau (Penguin Classics, 1983).

Gandhi: A Manga Biography by Kazuki Ebine (Penguin Books, 2011).

Gandhi: An Illustrated Biography by Pramod Kapoor (Black Dog & Leventhal, 2017).

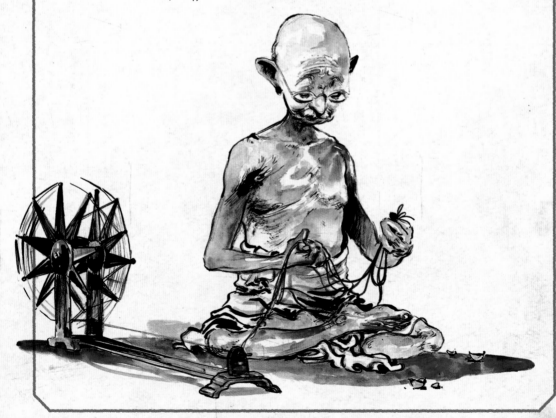

SEEDS
OFPEACE

All twenty-eight of the creators of this book have agreed to donate their work so that all of their proceeds can go to Seeds of Peace, an organization that we feel embodies Gandhi's mission.

Seeds of Peace inspires and cultivates new generations of global leaders in communities divided by conflict, equipping them with the skills and relationships they need to accelerate social, economic, and political changes essential to peace.

Seeds of Peace's approach focuses on three types of change: personal and interpersonal transformation, and wider societal change.

Its leadership development model begins with a transformational camp session in the United States for exceptional young people and educators living in conflict. The program shifts attitudes and perceptions and builds respect and empathy.

The approach continues through year-round local programs that strengthen relationships and leadership capacities, and strives to accelerate the impact of their alumni who are challenging the ideologies, policies, and practices that perpetuate conflict.

The Seeds of Peace network includes thousands of alumni throughout the Middle East, South Asia, Europe, and the United States who are uniquely positioned to lead change.

LEARN MORE AT WWW.SEEDSOFPEACE.ORG

Contributors

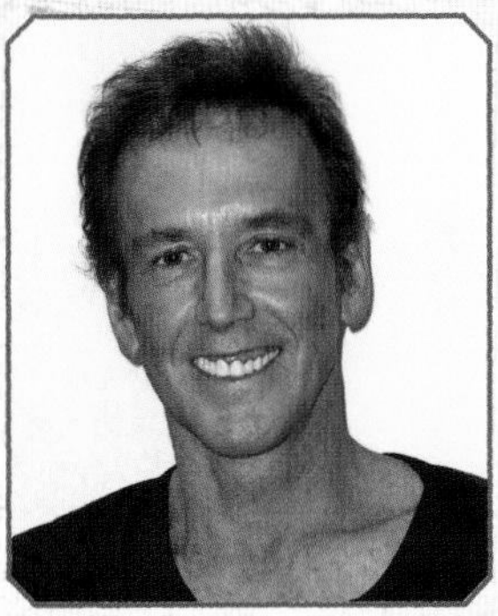

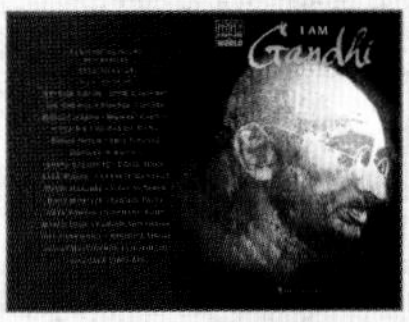
I AM
Gandhi

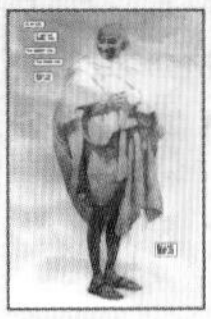

BILL SIENKIEWICZ | Bill Sienkiewicz is an Emmy-nominated, award-winning artist/author. He is perhaps best known for redefining the visual language and the public's perception of Comics as an Artform, by his use of innovative multimedia techniques and approaches, both analog and digital. He continues to influence new generations of creators. He also produces work in film, TV, animation, and music, and has exhibited worldwide.

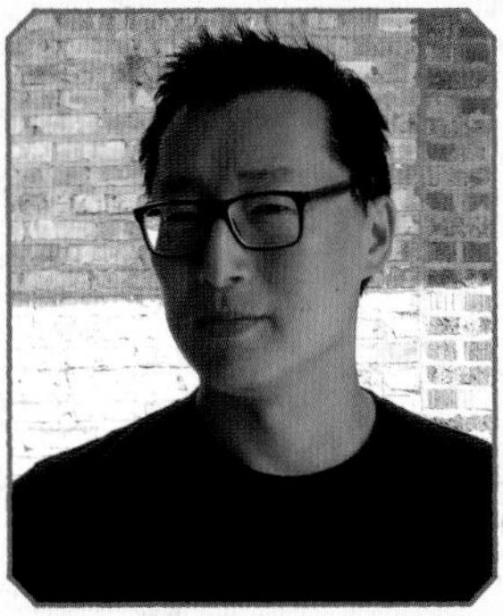

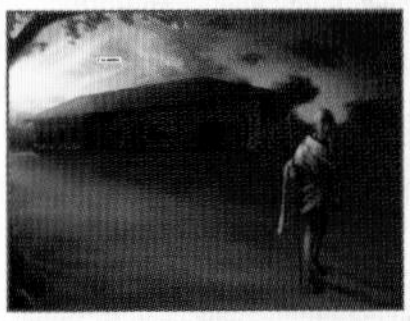

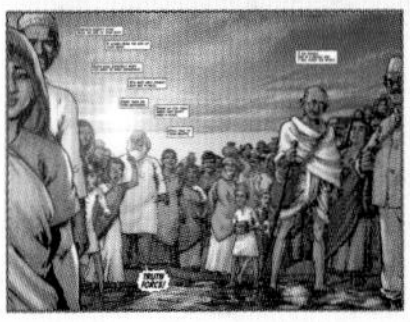

GENE HA | *New York Times* bestselling comic book artist Gene Ha writes and draws the comic book *Mae*. He is best known for his work with writer Alan Moore, *Top 10* and its prequel, *The Forty-Niners*. Both projects won Eisners, the highest award in American comics. In 2008 he won his fourth Eisner for *Justice League of America* #11 with Brad Meltzer. Gene lives outside Chicago in Berwyn, Illinois with his lovely wife, Lisa.

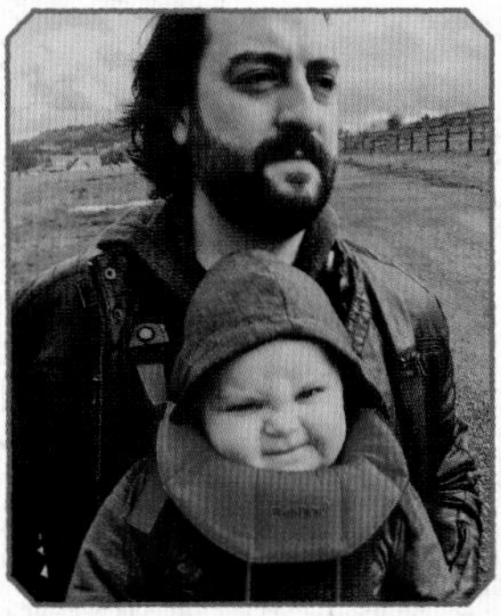

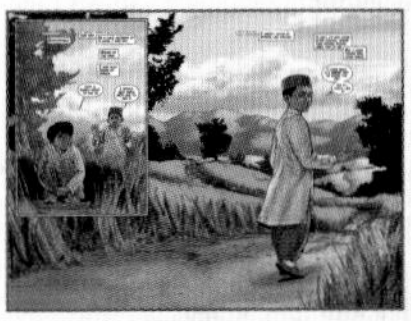

DAVID MARQUEZ | David Marquez is an Eisner Award–nominated comic book artist whose work includes the *New York Times* bestselling *Miles Morales: The Ultimate Spider-Man*, *All-New X-Men*, *Invincible Iron Man*, *Civil War II*, and *The Defenders*, as well as his first creator-owned graphic novel *The Joyners in 3D*. He lives in Portland, Oregon, with his wife, son, and two dogs.

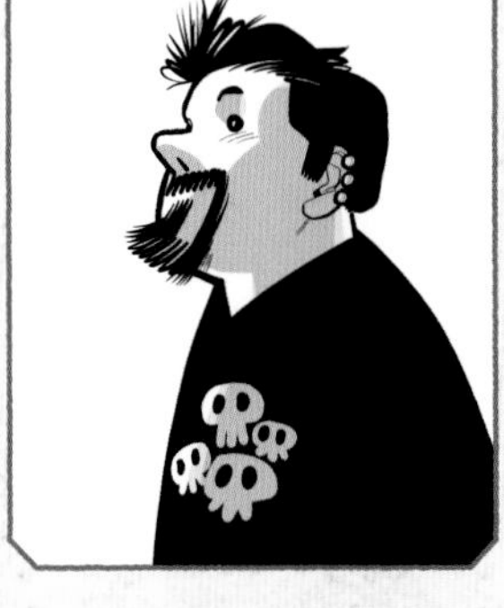

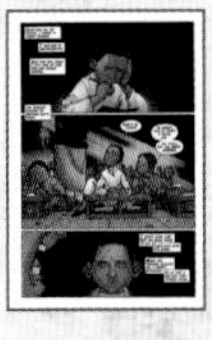

DAVID LAFUENTE | Born in Spain, David Lafuente first broke into the U.S. comic industry in 2008 when he drew the sleeper hit miniseries *Patsy Walker: Hellcat*. Best known for his work on *Ultimate Spider-Man* and Neil Gaiman's *The Graveyard Book*, he is currently working on a creator-owned book written by Kieron Gillen and Jim Rossignol.

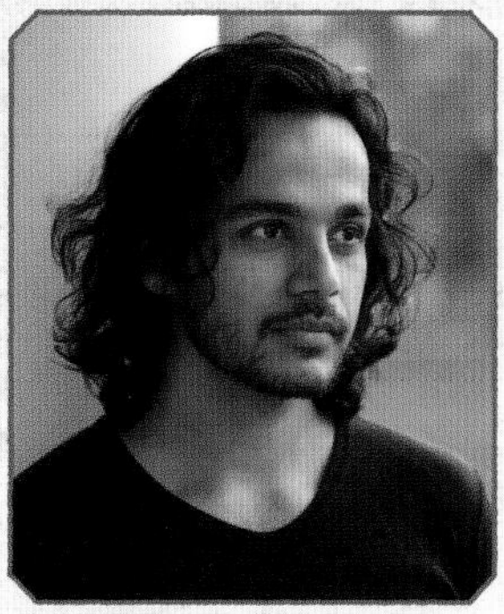

ABHISHEK SINGH | Abhishek Singh's comic books, including Deepak Chopra & Shekhar Kapur's *Ramayan 3392 A.D.*, have been translated into numerous languages. His critically acclaimed *Krishna: A Journey Within* is the first graphic novel by an Indian author/illustrator to be released by an American comic book publisher. In addition to comics, he has worked on animated and virtual reality films, and his art has been exhibited widely.

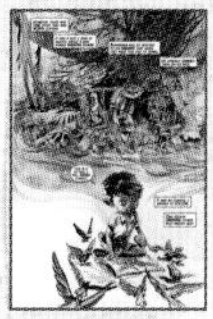

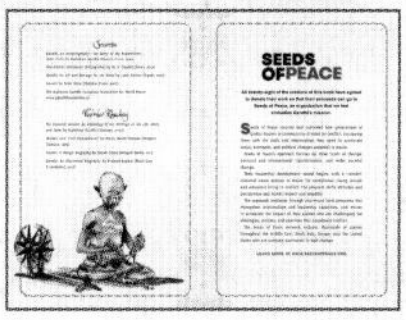
SEEDS OF PEACE

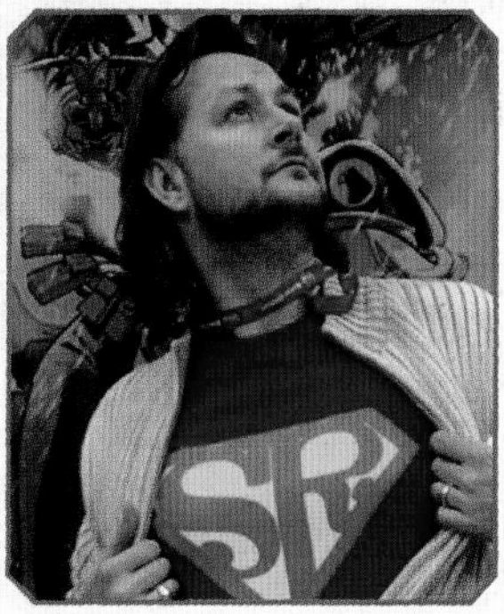

STEPHANE ROUX | Stephane Roux is a French illustrator best known for his cover artwork for Marvel, Semic, and DC Comics, although he has also dabbled in music, sculpting, animation, and graphic novels. His most notable projects include *Birds of Prey*, *X-Men: Worlds Apart*, *The Amazing Spider-Man*, *Batman*, *Zatanna*, *Star Wars*, *Harley Quinn* and *Powergirl* miniseries.

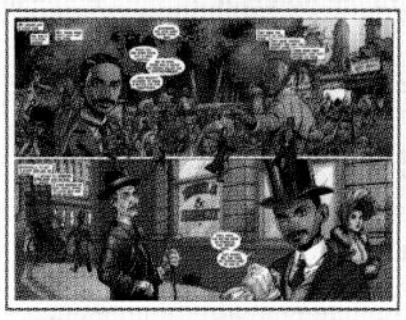

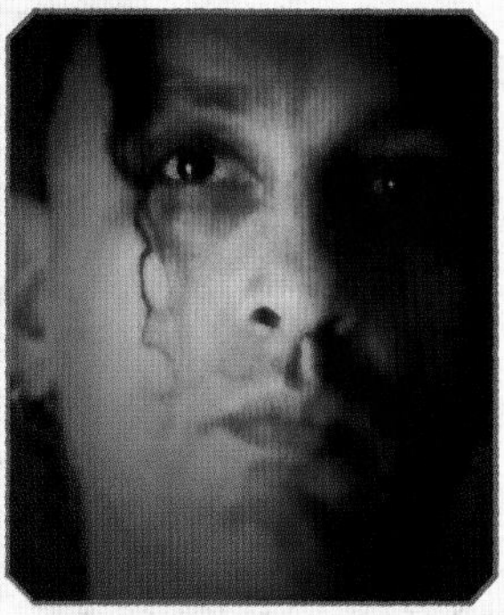

RAGS MORALES | Rags Morales started his comic book career working on comics based on TSR's Dungeons and Dragons games, and has since worked on numerous comic books by such luminary writers as Harlan Ellison, Grant Morrison, and Tim Truman. He has been published by DC Comics, Dark Horse, and Marvel Comics. His favorite project to date was the bestselling *Identity Crisis* by Brad Meltzer. A father of four, he lives in Pennsylvania.

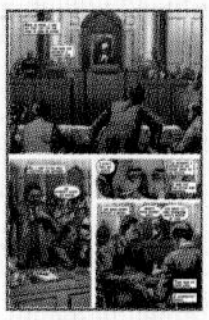

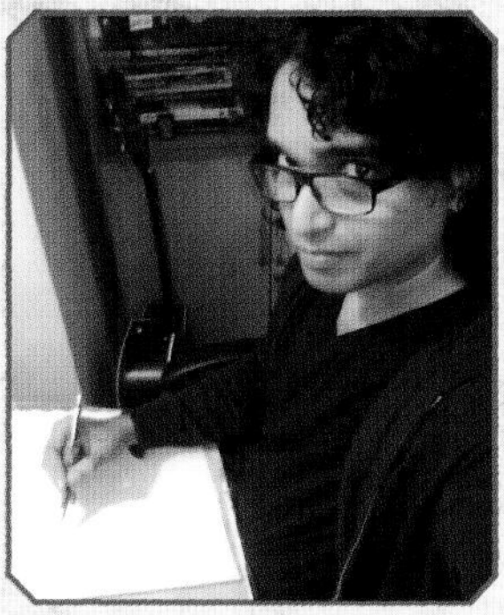

SIDDHARTH KOTIAN | Sid Kotian is a comic book artist from Mumbai, India. His previous works include collaborations with Eisner Award–winning writer J. Michael Straczynski. Currently Sid is working with Matt Doyle and Beth Behrs on the popular webcomic *Dents*.

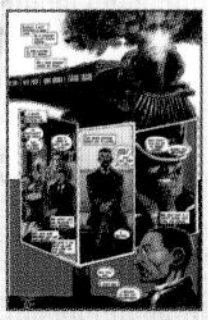

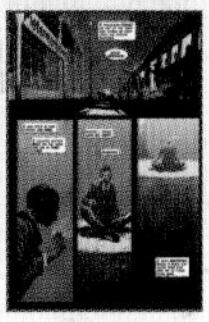

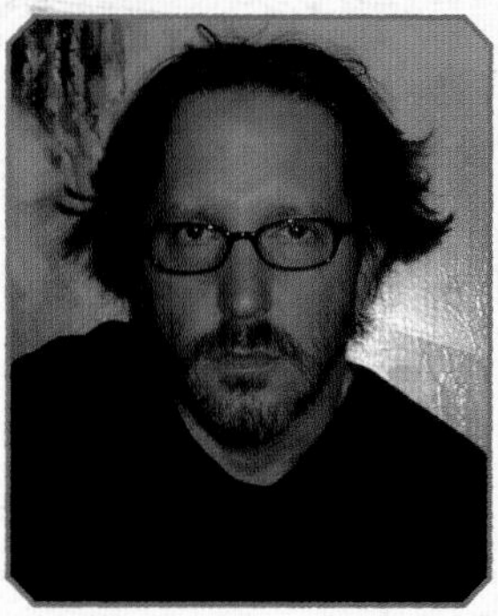

MICHAEL GAYDOS | Michael Gaydos has worked in the comic and graphic novel world for the past twenty years. His credits include projects for Marvel, DC, Archie, Dark Circle, Dark Horse, Image, IDW, NBC, and more. He has received two Eisner Award nominations for his work on *Alias* with Brian Michael Bendis, and he is a co-creator of Marvel's *Jessica Jones*. In addition, Michael's fine art has been the subject of a number of solo exhibitions and can be found in private collections worldwide.

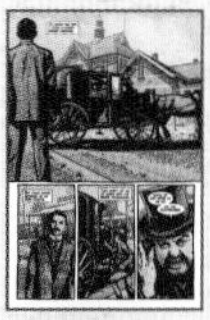

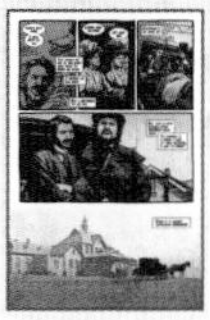

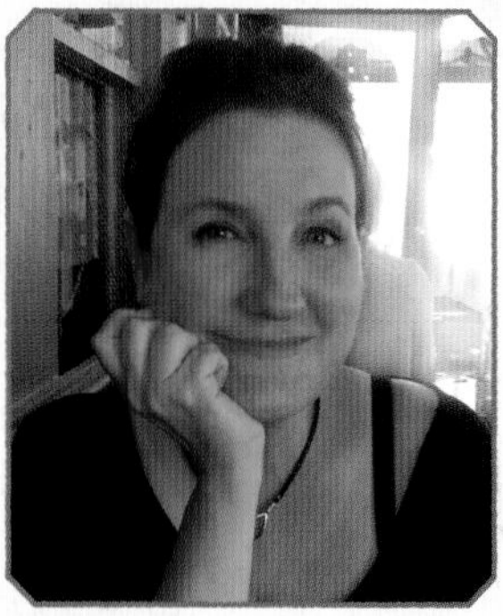

AMANDA CONNER | Award-winning artist Amanda Conner began her career in advertising, and has since illustrated many of the top comics in the field, including *Supergirl*, *Painkiller Jane*, *Wonder Woman*, *Powergirl*, *Terra*, and *Gatecrasher*. She was the co-writer and artist, along with Darwyn Cooke, for *Before Watchmen: Silk Spectre,* and since has worked with her husband co-writing and illustrating *Harley Quinn* for DC Comics. Her art has been featured on shows such as *Nightline* and *Big Bang Theory*.

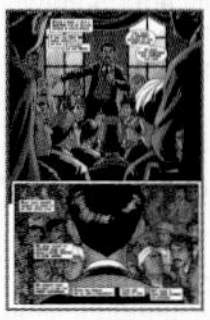

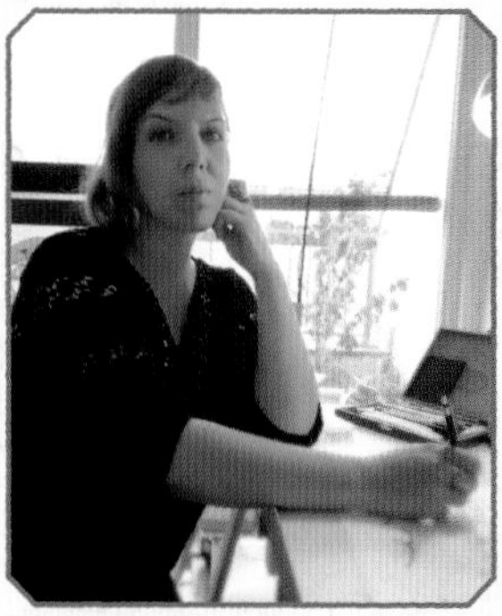

STEPHANIE HANS | French illustrator Stephanie Hans has worked on book covers and numerous comics for DC, Dark Horse, and Marvel, including *Batman*, *Batwoman*, *Angela: Queen of Hel*, *Generations*, and *Deadman*.

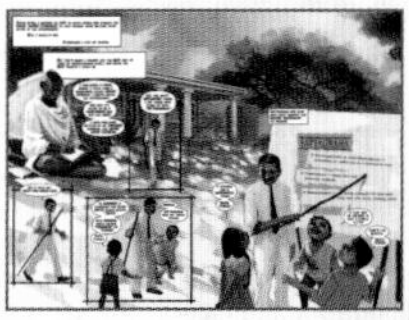

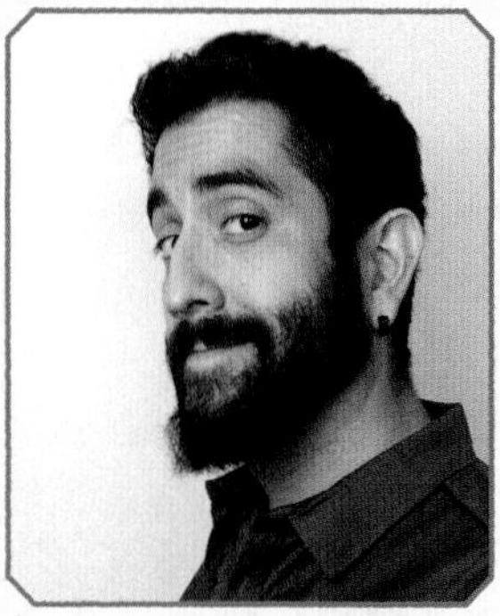

CARLOS D'ANDA | Carlos D'Anda joined Jim Lee's Wildstorm Studios in his late teens, originally as an illustrator and concept artist. Since, he has gone on to draw numerous comics, including *WildCats*, *Bionicle*, *Deathblow*, *Batman*, *Star Wars*, *JLA*, and most recently, an issue of DC's *Kamandi Challenge*. He has also worked on the design and art direction of a number of video and online games. Carlos lives in San Diego.

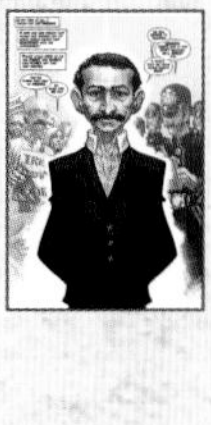

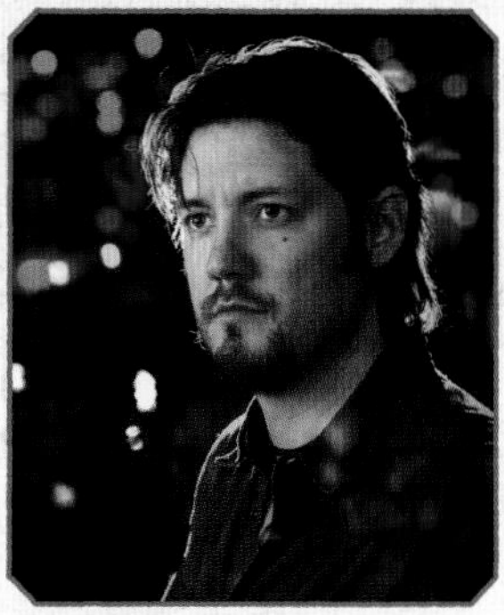

JOHN CASSADAY | A native Texan, John Cassaday has called New York City home since 1997. He is best known for his work on the critically acclaimed DC Comics series *Planetary* with writer Warren Ellis, *Astonishing X-Men* with writer Joss Whedon, and the relaunch of *Star Wars* with writer Jason Aaron. He has also worked in advertising and film, and made his directorial debut on Joss Whedon's TV series *Dollhouse*. His work has been exhibited around the world.

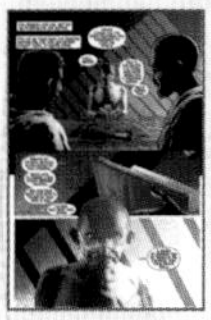

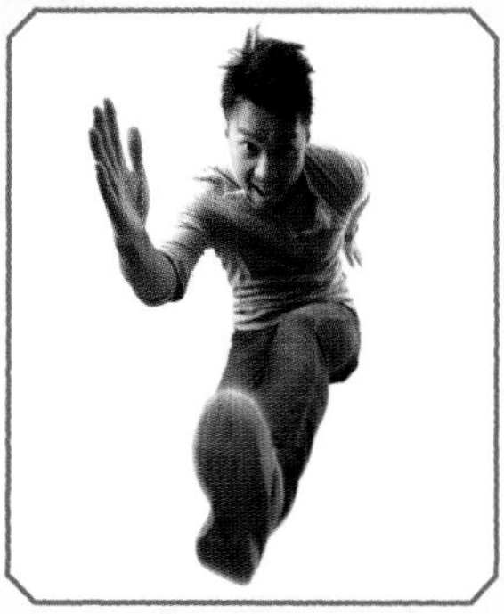

FRANCIS MANAPUL | Francis Manapul is a *New York Times* bestselling and award-winning artist and writer based in Toronto, Canada. He is best known for his work relaunching *The Flash* for DC Comics, followed by the company's namesake title, *Detective Comics*. He is currently the writer and artist of the DC Rebirth title *Trinity*, and his past work includes *Superman/Batman*, *Legion of Super-Heroes*, and a prolific career as a cover artist. He was a host on History Channel's *Beast Legends*.

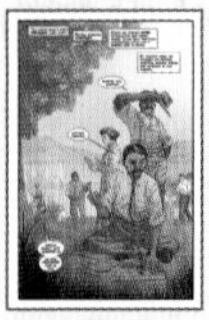

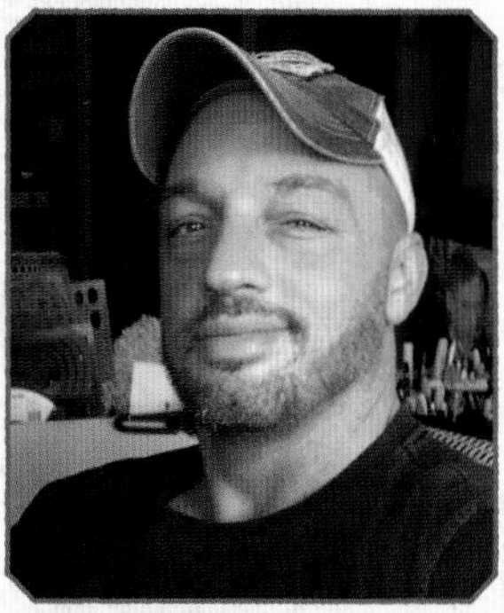

PHIL JIMENEZ | Phil Jimenez is an award-winning writer and artist best known for his work on *Tempest*, *The Invisibles*, *New X-Men*, *Wonder Woman*, *Infinite Crisis*, *Amazing Spider-Man*, *The Transformers*, *DC: Rebirth*, and *Superwoman*. Jimenez has also worked in film, television, print media, and product design, has lectured at universities and museums, and teaches at SVA and CCA. He is considered one of the most prominent gay creators in mainstream comics.

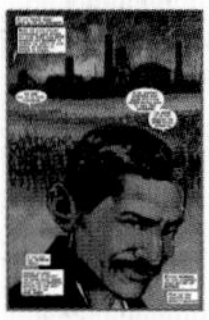

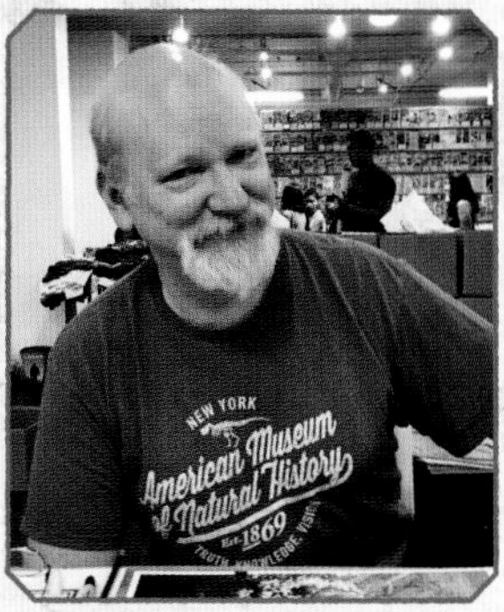
NEW YORK
American Museum of Natural History
EST. 1869

ARTHUR ADAMS | Arthur "Art" Adams is an award-winning comic artist whose decades-long career has included work on such titles as *Batman*, *Superman*, *Avengers*, *Spider-Man*, *X-Men*, *New Mutants*, *Godzilla*, *Danger Girl*, *Excalibur*, *Guardians of the Galaxy*, *Hulk*, and his first big success at age nineteen, *Longshot*. He's the creator, writer, and artist of *Monkeyman and O'Brien*. Outside of comics, Art has done movie, toy, book illustrations, and provided the artwork for an X-Men–themed Spaghetti-O's can.

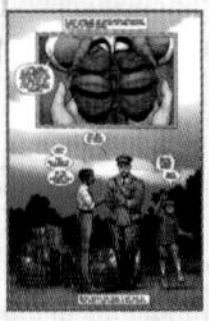

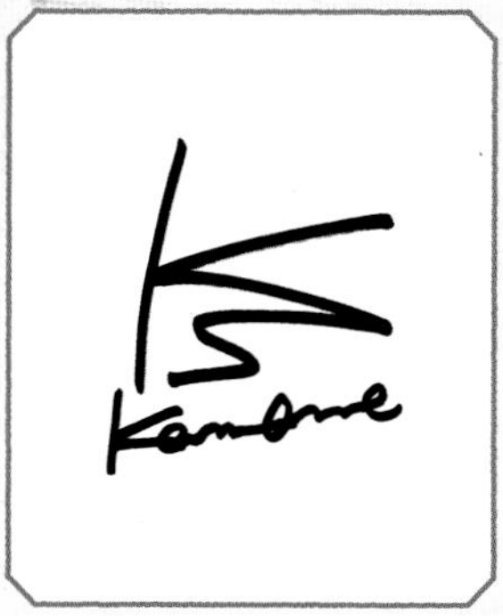

KAMOME SHIRAHAMA | Japanese illustrator Kamome Shirahama has been working as a freelance illustrator and manga-ka (manga artist) since graduating from art school. Her recent works include *Atelier of Witch Hat* and covers for *Doctor Aphra*, *Batgirl*, and *Birds of Prey*.

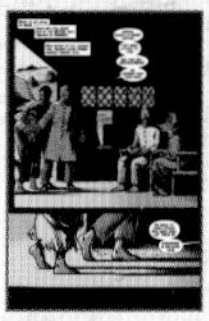

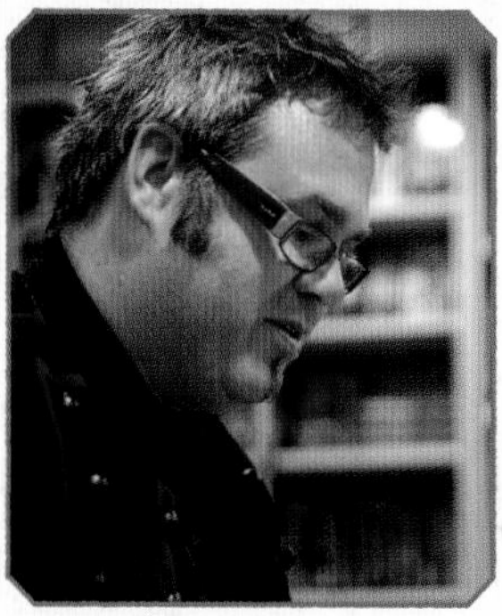

BRYAN HITCH | Bryan Hitch is a British artist who has illustrated numerous comics for DC and Marvel. He is known for his work on *The Authority*, *Captain America: Reborn*, *The Ultimates*, and *Justice League of America*, and he is the author and artist of the creator-owned series *Real Heroes*. His artwork and designs have appeared in direct-to-video animated films, television, and major feature films, such as the 2009 film *Star Trek*.

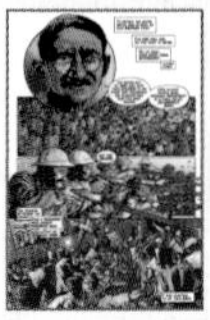

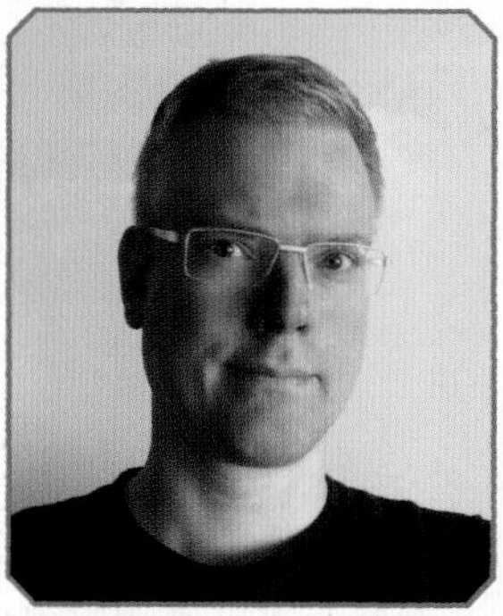

STEVE MCNIVEN | Steve McNiven has been drawing comic books for Marvel for over a decade. He is most acclaimed for his work with Mark Millar on the Marvel *Civil War* and *Old Man Logan* comic book series, both of which have influenced their movie counterparts. He is also well known (at home) for his work as a dad, husband, and avid cat lover.

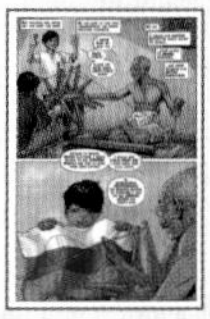

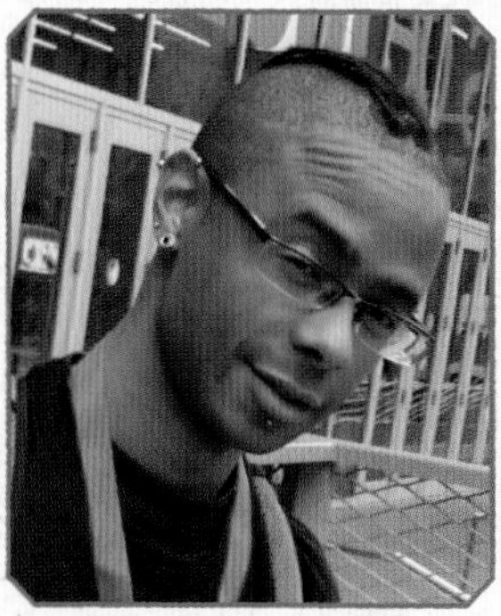

MARCO RUDY | Originally from Mozambique, Marco Rudy moved to Brazil and broke into comics by networking through his Deviant Art page. He has worked with DC and Marvel on such comics as *Superboy*, *Supergirl*, *Superman/Batman*, *Action Comics*, *Marvel Knights: Spider-Man*, *Uncanny X-Men*, *New Avengers Annual*, and *The Winter Soldier*. He is currently working on *Iron Man: Generations* and a creator-owned project.

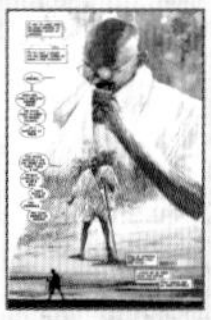

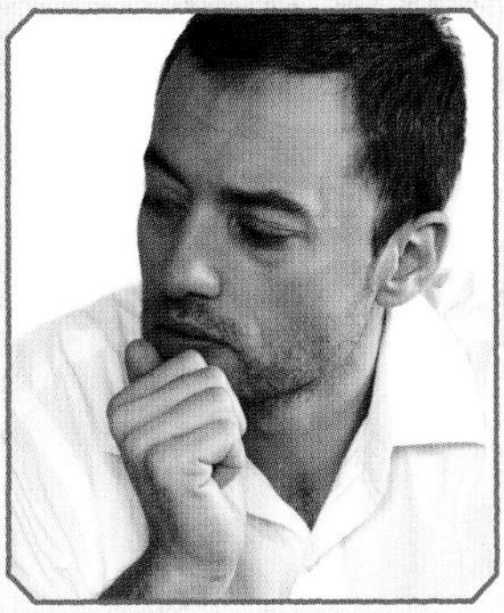

ALEX MALEEV | Born in 1971, Alex Maleev is an Eisner Award–winning Bulgarian illustrator with a fine arts background. He has often collaborated with Brian Michael Bendis, working on comics such as *Daredevil*, *Spider-Woman*, and *Halo: Uprising*; they are currently working on the creator-owned comic *Scarlet*. He also created the artwork for the character Sylar on the TV show *Heroes*.

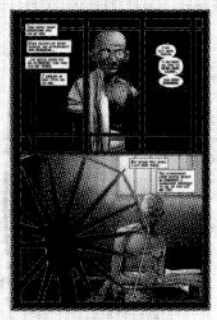

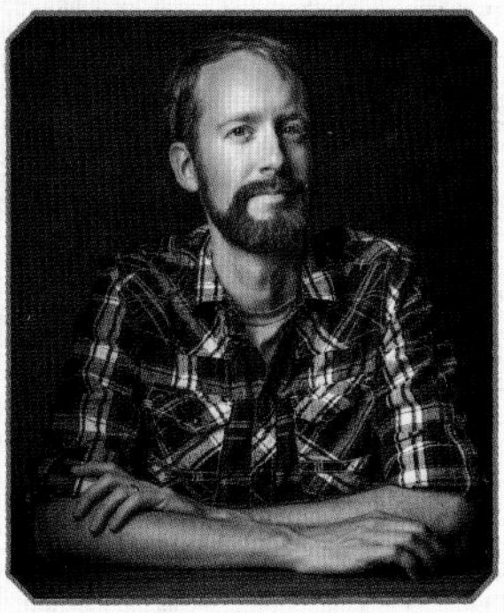

NATE POWELL | Nate Powell is the only cartoonist to have won a National Book Award, which he received for John Lewis's *March*. He began self-publishing at age fourteen and graduated from the School of Visual Arts in 2000. He has won two Eisner Awards and the Michael L. Printz Award, among other honors. Born in Little Rock, Arkansas, he now lives in Bloomington, Indiana.

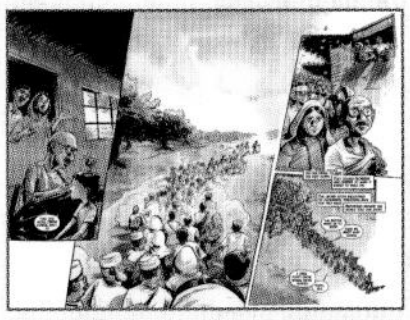

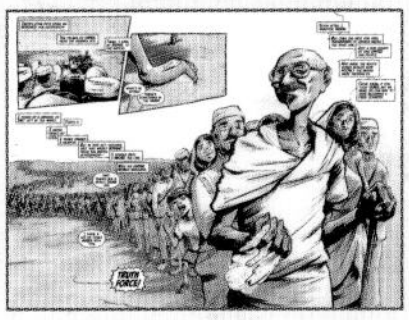

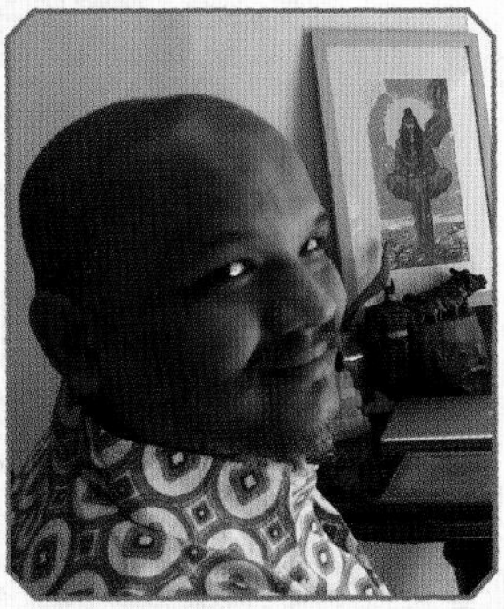

SAUMIN PATEL | Saumin Suresh Patel is a illustrator and concept artist living in Mumbai, India. He has worked for such clients as Virgin Comics, MTV, VH1, Grey, and Saatchi & Saatchi. He self-published his first book, *Kaamotsav Vol. 1*, in 2015, and is currently working on new comic book projects.

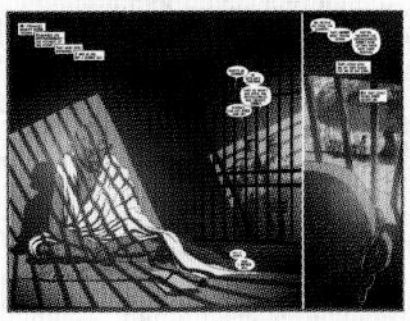

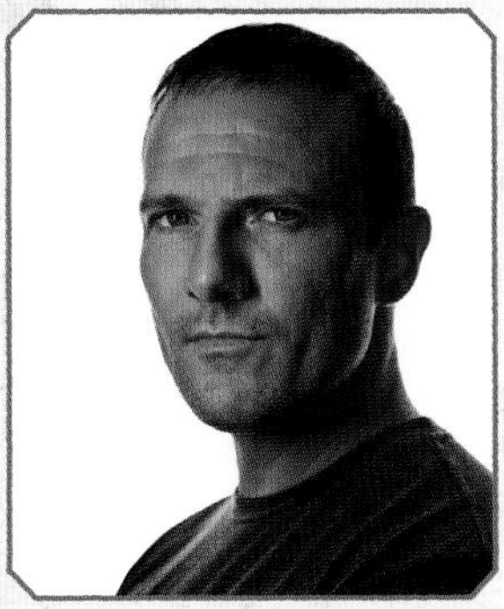

DAVID MACK | David Mack is the Emmy-nominated, Eisner Award–winning, *New York Times* bestselling author and artist of the *Kabuki* series, author of Marvel's *Daredevil*, cover artist of Neil Gaiman's *American Gods*, album cover artist for Paul McCartney, and artist for the opening titles of *Jessica Jones* and *Captain America: The Winter Soldier*. He is a Comic Book Ambassador of Arts & Story for the U.S. State Department, and his art has been exhibited in museums and galleries around the world.

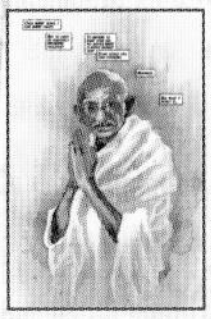

JIM CHEUNG | Jim Cheung is an exclusive penciler for Marvel Comics, who has most recently worked on *Spider-Man: Dead No More* and *Astonishing X-Men*. He is the co-creator of *Young Avengers* and *Scion*, has worked on titles such as *Avengers vs X-Men*, *New Avengers*, *Uncanny X-Men*, *Illuminati*, and *Iron Man*, and has created illustrations for *the New York Times,* ESPN, the *Village Voice*, and more.

BRAD MELTZER | Brad Meltzer is the #1 *New York Times* best-selling author of *The Inner Circle* and ten other best-selling thrillers. His newest book is *The Escape Artist*. He is also the author of the Ordinary People Change the World series of picture book biographies (which includes *I am Gandhi*, the younger version of this book), one of the people who helped save Superman's house, and is the host of the History Channel television shows *Decoded* and *Lost History* (in which he helped find the missing 9/11 flag). He lives in Florida with his wife and their three children.

ALEX SINCLAIR | Alex Sinclair has worked in the comic book industry as a colorist for almost twenty-five years. Most of his career has been spent coloring for DC Comics and their many characters, including *Batman*, *Wonder Woman*, *Justice League,* and *Superman*. His collaborations with Jim Lee and Scott Williams on *Batman Hush*, and Ivan Reis and Joe Prado on *Blackest Night* earned him global recognition and multiple awards. Alex lives in San Diego with his wife, Rebecca, and daughters, Grace, Blythe, Meredith, and Harley.

CHRISTOPHER ELIOPOULOS | Christopher Eliopoulos has worked in every aspect of comic book creation. He's known as a prolific letterer, and has been nominated for Eisner and Harvey Awards for the comics he has written and illustrated, such as *Cow Boy* and *Franklin Richards: Son of a Genius*. He is the illustrator of the *New York Times* best-selling Ordinary People Change the World picture book series by Brad Meltzer, and the author/illustrator of the graphic novel *Cosmic Commandos*. He lives in New Jersey with his wife and their identical twin sons (when the boys are home from college).

Introduce the young people in your life to these engaging and accessible picture book biographies

I am Amelia Earhart
BRAD MELTZER
Illustrated by Christopher Eliopoulos
I am Abraham Lincoln
BRAD MELTZER
Illustrated by Christopher Eliopoulos
I am Rosa Parks
BRAD MELTZER
Illustrated by Christopher Eliopoulos
I am Albert Einstein
BRAD MELTZER
Illustrated by Christopher Eliopoulos
I am Jackie Robinson
BRAD MELTZER
Illustrated by Christopher Eliopoulos
I am Lucille Ball
BRAD MELTZER
Illustrated by Christopher Eliopoulos
I am Martin Luther King, Jr.
BRAD MELTZER
Illustrated by Christopher Eliopoulos
I am Helen Keller
BRAD MELTZER
Illustrated by Christopher Eliopoulos
I am George Washington
BRAD MELTZER
Illustrated by Christopher Eliopoulos
I am Jane Goodall
I am Jim Henson
BRAD MELTZER
Illustrated by Christopher Eliopoulos
I am Sacagawea
BRAD MELTZER
Illustrated by Christopher Eliopoulos
I am
BRAD MELTZER
Christopher Eliopoulos
I am Harriet Tubman
BRAD MELTZER
Illustrated by Christopher Eliopoulos

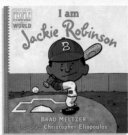

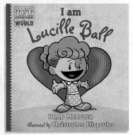

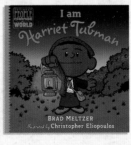

We can all be heroes!

For Jill Kneerim,
wise soul,
great soul

Special thanks to my heroes—all the artists who gave their
precious time to make this book possible. Thanks also to Marc Andreyko,
Brian Michael Bendis, Tom Brevoort, Dan DiDio, Diane Nelson, Nick
Marell, Aki Yanagi, and all our friends at DC and Marvel who opened
their contact lists and helped us pull this inspiring group together.
Alex Sinclair, you are the greatest colorist ever. Extra thanks to
Colleen Ring and Reva Joshee of the Mahatma Gandhi
Canadian Foundation for World Peace for their input on
early drafts. And finally, extra love to Chris Eliopoulos,
who is truly my brother—and who killed himself
on this for no other reason than
the mission.
—B.M.

DIAL BOOKS
An imprint of Penguin Random House LLC
375 Hudson Street, New York, NY 10014

ISBN 9780525552697
Photo of Gandhi at the spinning wheel on page 39 by Popperfoto courtesy of Getty Images

Printed in China • 10 9 8 7 6 5 4 3 2 1
Designed by Jason Henry
Text set in Triplex

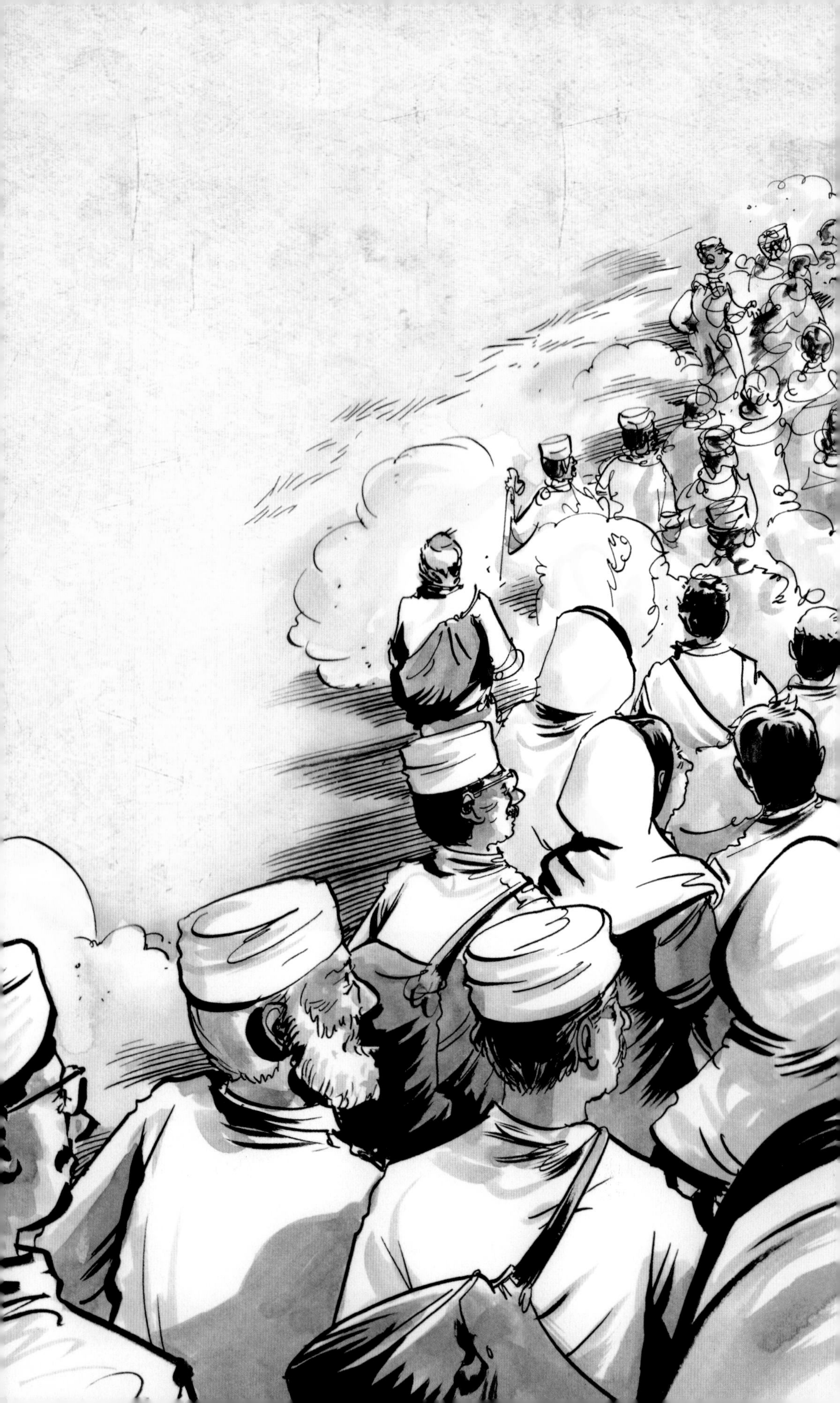

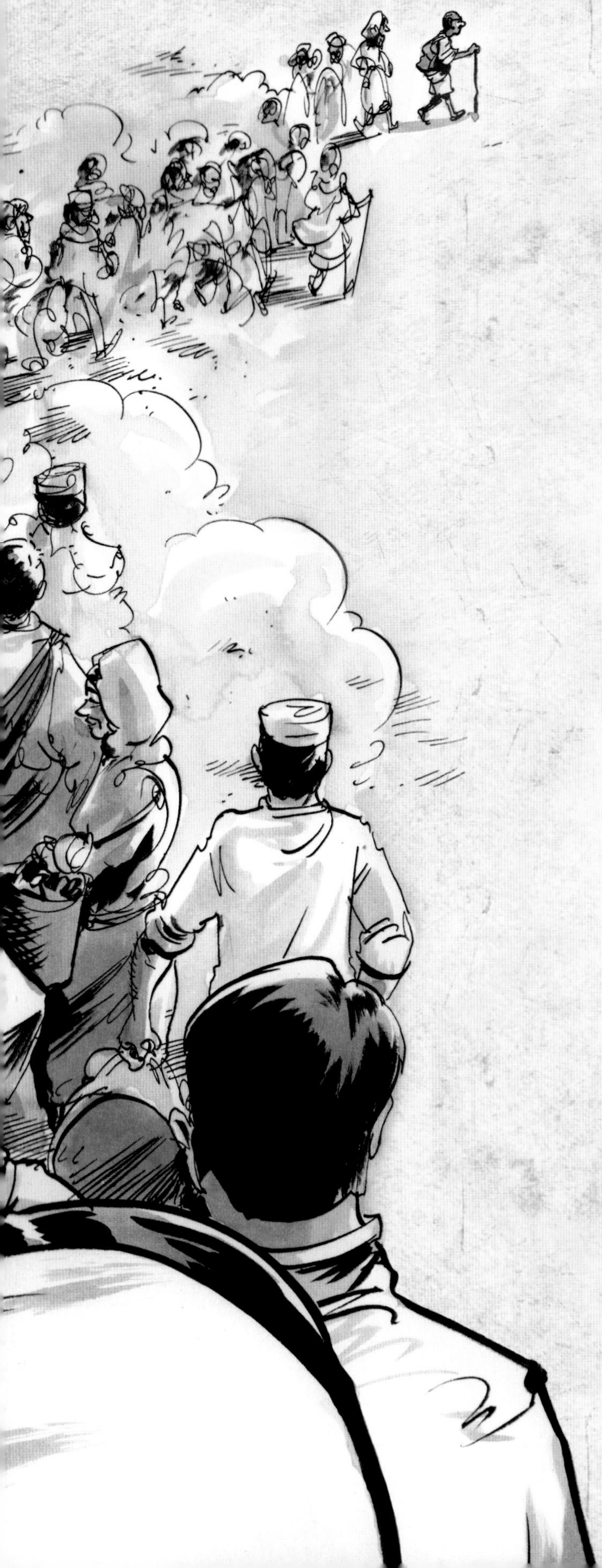

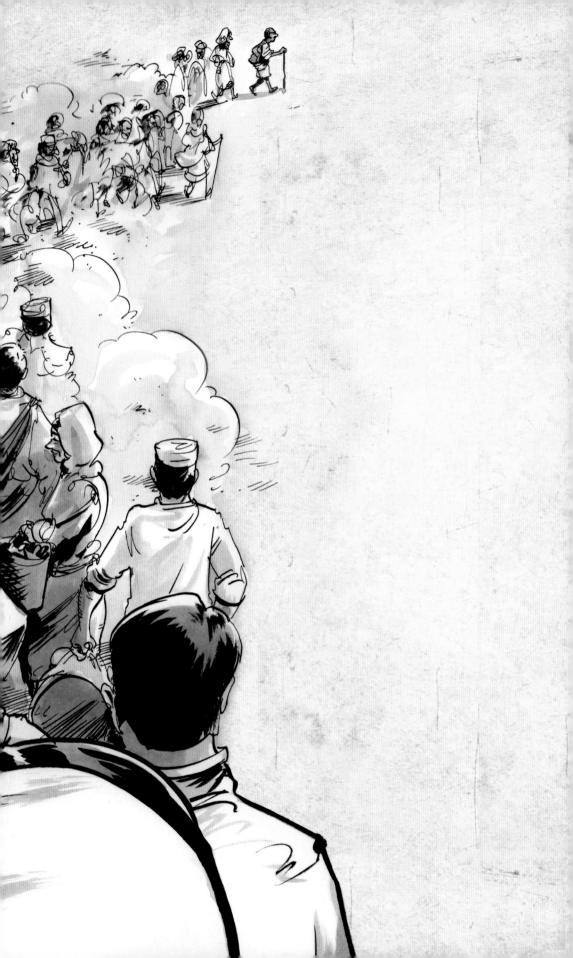